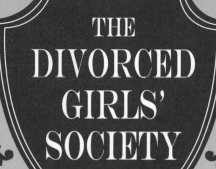

THE
DIVORCED
GIRLS'
SOCIETY

Your Initiation into the Club
You Never Thought You'd Join

VICKI KING AND
JENNIFER O'CONNELL

POLKA DOT
press ®

The Polka Dot Press® name and logo design are registered
trademarks of F+W Publications, Inc.

Published by Adams Media, an F+W Publications Company
57 Littlefield Street
Avon, MA 02322
www.adamsmedia.com

ISBN-10: 1-59869-162-7
ISBN-13: 978-1-59869-162-7

Library of Congress Cataloging-in-Publication Data
King, Vicki.
The divorced girls' society /
Vicki King and Jennifer O'Connell.
p. cm.
Includes index.
ISBN-13: 978-1-59869-162-7 (pbk.)
ISBN-10: 1-59869-162-7 (pbk.)
1. Divorced women—Life skills guides. I. O'Connell,
Jennifer. II. Title.
HQ814.K56 2007
306.89'3—dc22   2007018898

Printed in Canada.
J I H G F E D C B A

This publication is designed to provide accurate and authoritative information with regard to the subject matter covered. It is sold with the understanding that the publisher is not engaged in rendering legal, accounting, or other professional advice. If legal advice or other expert assistance is required, the services of a competent professional person should be sought.

—From a *Declaration of Principles* jointly adopted by a Committee of the American Bar Association and a Committee of Publishers and Associations

Many of the designations used by manufacturers and sellers to distinguish their product are claimed as trademarks. Where those designations appear in this book and Adams Media was aware of a trademark claim, the designations have been printed with initial capital letters.

This book is available at quantity discounts for bulk purchases.
For information, please call 1-800-289-0963.

For D.S.T.
—V.K.K.

Because the odds were against us and twelve years
later he still makes me smile, for John.
—J.L.O.

Acknowledgments

Thanks to our agent, Kristin Nelson, and editor, Jennifer Kushnier, for recognizing that smart, divorcing women need an owner's manual, and that two points of view make it even better. To Vangie Deane, who rounds out our trifecta, for lending her ears and giving us her relevant perspective. And thanks to the owner of the small cottage in Edgartown where we stayed that sunny weekend in October 2006 and had our most brilliant literary moments.

Contents

Introduction

I bet you never thought you'd be reading a book about divorce, right? You were supposed to be one of that lucky 50 percent who stayed married forever; half of that golden couple from the DeBeers commercial, the woman who strolls off into the sunset holding the hand of her life partner (only in the commercial you have one hell of a rock on that hand, too).

But now, instead of counting carats you're counting your lawyer's hourly rate. And while a diamond may be forever, an hour with your attorney is $325. Welcome to the club.

Welcome to the Divorced Girls' Society.

You probably have a mental list of clubs you never thought you'd join: the Hair Club for Women, the Beanie Baby of the Month Club, Cuticle Biters Anonymous. But being divorced, while possibly unexpected and probably a last resort, is not something to be ashamed of, something you're forced to admit in a church-basement meeting room, surrounded by Krispy Kremes. Divorce doesn't discriminate—we're all free game. But in the Divorced Girls' Society, you have a place where you can feel like you belong, like you're not alone.

With the Divorced Girls' Society, you have officially entered a judgment-free zone. I'm not here to assign blame, offer excuses, or help you decide who really deserves to keep that antique side table Aunt Gladys bequeathed to you on her deathbed. It doesn't matter who decided to call it quits, and, in the grand scheme of things, it certainly doesn't matter who ends up with a musty-smelling side table. The fact is, you're getting divorced. And what matters is helping you come out healthier, happier, and hopeful—yes, you can actually have hope!—on the other side.

The Divorced Girls' Society doesn't pull any punches. I don't just proclaim to know what it's like to go through a divorce—I've actually been there. I lived through the late night phone calls, the endless e-mails, and daily check-ins where an unanswered phone set off my own version of an Amber alert. And not only did I survive to tell about it, I actually lived to find the humor in the situation (yes, there is some humor, although sometimes you have to look really, really hard to find it). There were even a few "a-ha" moments, those flashes of recognition when you realize you've actually made some progress and you experience a bonafide watershed moment. Like the first time you ask your ex how he's doing and, instead of feigning interest while you secretly imagine him tied to a railroad track like those old-fashioned damsels in distress, you actually care to hear the answer. Or when you have to pause for a few seconds to remember your wedding date. Or when you can look back on moments when you were married and think that there were some good times after all. And there had to be, right?

When I was going through "the big D," I desperately wished for divorce advice, girlfriend style. I wanted someone to hold the ropes tight on the swinging bridge that was testing my balance, not to mention my ability to keep down a meal. I wanted to find someone wise enough to help me get through what was shaping up to be a pretty miserable experience. So I hit the bookstores in search of advice, perspective, and a glimpse of what to expect on the road ahead. And, after unsuccessfully navigating numerous aisles and discovering there's actually a market for books on easy dessert recipes for recovering bulimics, I found myself in a section that implied I might be capable of helping myself. Imagine that, little old me! After all, who knows me better?

After waiting until the aisle cleared and all bystanders (read: witnesses) were gone, I made my move. And there, in the self-help aisle, I did, indeed, discover that there is plenty written about divorce by authors with all sorts of impressive credentials. The problem was, once I read the book jackets and scanned through the chapters, I didn't feel like they were talking *to* me; they were talking *at* me. At times preachy, condescending, talking in metaphors and similes, or screaming at me like a deranged JV soccer coach, with me the slacker bench warmer. Other times, the advice was so damn *sensitive*, so mild mannered and squishy, I feared the book would include a group hug and a recitation of "Kumbaya." I couldn't make heads or tails of what this had to do with my divorce. Or, I had a hard time buying into it because, while I was impressed by the string of degrees and letters following the author's name, I was less than impressed with the author's ability to put himself in my shoes. I wanted to listen, really I did. I wanted someone to help guide me, someone who understood what I was going through and who understood me, not someone with a fancy degree or an expertise in relationships—after all, the whole reason I was visiting that aisle was that I was no longer *in* a relationship.

I needed the cold, hard facts, with a heaping teaspoon of humor. I needed information that was practical, and help expecting the proverbial unexpected. And wouldn't it be nice if it were enhanced with the perspective of my girlfriend? One who could pick up on the most subtle of behaviors, read me like a book, and react appropriately. I needed the divorce expert and the savvy girlfriend to partner with me on my journey. And not just any girlfriend, by the way; I needed one who could dig in her heels with me to battle this strange and unknown universe. I needed the kind of girlfriend who will tell you when your favorite black skirt should be retired, but makes it all better by joining you on a shopping spree for a new one. After all, a good girlfriend knows you better than any self-help book.

This is where my best friend, Jennifer, comes in. You can always find a good lawyer or family therapist, but it is your friends who bear witness to your struggle and put a marital crisis into the larger context of your life. Because she helped me get through my divorce with such flying colors, I thought you could use her help, too. This book, then, can actually be divided into two perspectives. When you come across sidebars, you'll be getting an entirely new perspective on the situation: Jennifer's. The best friend's. Joining the Divorced Girls' Society is not only getting the lowdown on how you, the divorcing woman, can manage to turn lemons into lemonade (or at least a lemon-drop martini), it's also about how your close girlfriends can help you move ahead. Jennifer will pipe in frequently with her two cents in sections called "What Your Girlfriend Is Thinking," because you need a friend when your marriage ends, someone who knows you—sometimes better than you know yourself. And while you're learning how to navigate the heady waters of divorce, she'll provide some tips to help your friends help you, and let you in on what they're thinking. And believe me, they're thinking a lot.

We want to help take those thoughts and turn them into positive-action steps. So we'll give you tips, in sections called "Tips for Your Speed-Dial Sisters," on how to help your girlfriends help you, and give you advice on how to handle the sticky friendship situations that are bound to creep up as you both wade into uncharted waters. These tips are reserved for your closest friends. You know the kind: the friends who loved you when you thought blue eyeliner and a spiral perm were great ideas. They stuck by you through the jean jacket with the embroidered Bon Jovi logo on the back. And they didn't turn a cold shoulder when, after one too many tequila shots, you Googled your high school boyfriend and then called the monastery to proclaim your undying love for Brother Carl. They're your best girlfriends, and if you've ever needed them, this is the time. And because we recognize that even with the best of intentions, our friends flounder in the face of our divorce, we include these Tips for Your Speed-Dial Sisters for when a girlfriend may not be certain as to what course of action to take.

Sometimes it might be hard to see that the glass is half full—especially when the glass is gone because your ex has packed up your favorite stemware for his new apartment without checking with you first. Divorce is a transition that forces you to develop strengths, recognize weaknesses, and embrace your (sometimes hidden) talents. Even if that talent is Academy Award–winning moments like feigning surprise when your ex complains that he's allergic to cats—and you just happen to have adopted a lovely long-haired named Mr. Whiskers.

Throughout the book, you'll see sidebars called "The Divorced Girls' Society Toolkit," where Jennifer and I will call out the practical, helpful tools that will come in handy in your day-to-day divorcing life. They'll help you make it through the first months, or (gulp) even years. Since they are set apart from the rest of the book, you'll have easy access to them and can refer to them in a jiffy.

Also peppered throughout this guide are "Mantras to Get You Through the Day"—simple phrases and thoughts that can make a huge difference in helping to put certain issues in perspective. These mantras peel away all of the complicated nonsense and get to the heart of what's important to remember when your brain can hardly remember what day it is during these emotionally taxing times. They aren't necessarily earth-shattering revelations, and they definitely don't require as much brain matter as learning the periodic table in high school chemistry, but these few words will keep you focused on the task at hand, and that's a giant step in the right direction.

While you'll get to read plenty of real stories—the good, the bad, and the ugly—I hope this book will also serve as a helpful guide. It's a resource you can pick up and put down, refer to again and again. Feel free to skip to chapters that address what you need to know at a particular time. Use the exercises when they make sense, and pass this book along to your girlfriends so they'll know when to nod in agreement and when to give you a cold hard dose of reality as you start to lean on them during your big life change.

There may be times when you'll think, *That's not the way it is for me,* and you're right; people don't always fit neatly into categories, stages, and twelve-step programs. But that's our point. In the end, everyone writes her own script. So take what applies and don't worry about what doesn't—it's how *you* decide to use the information that matters the most.

You can rest assured that this book is not written by some stuffy know-it-all (although I *do* like to think I know a lot, even if I'd hate to think I'm stuffy). I'm not a priest—my holier-than-thou days left me in the spring of my freshman year, when I discovered keg stands and pot-smoking frat boys. And I'm not a therapist. But I see one regularly, and would strongly recommend you get one, too. If you're looking for psychobabble and fancy theories or a step-by-step program, this isn't the place to find it. You also won't find some watered-down touchy-feely version of divorce provided by people with plenty of degrees on their walls, but no practical experience watching their husbands not only move into the spare bedroom, but actually rearrange the furniture, install a mini-fridge, *and* take the TV from the home office to enhance his living space.

You will have the benefit of my missteps and mistakes, the inside perspective on events that you haven't even considered, and the humorous recounting of some pretty embarrassing moments I lived through because I just didn't know better. Moreover, you'll have the girlfriend perspective, too—the advice and point of view of a critical player in this Superbowl of life-changing games.

As a pledge sister in the Divorced Girls' Society, you will feel empowered and supported, but we expect you to be a strong and willing pledge sister. It's hard to take a life that might be happening *to* you, and make it a life that happens on your own terms. But that's what the Divorce Girls' Society embodies—the belief that we divorcing women are, in spite of all of the messy stuff, the owners and keepers of our happiness. Jennifer and I are going to help you own it again, and set your life back on a course that is what you want it to be.

To paraphrase an old saying: Some women actively pursue divorce and others have it thrust upon them. Regardless of which camp you fall into, it's amazing how similar the experiences can be. As I was nearing the end of my own divorce experience, another of our friends was just beginning hers, albeit under different circumstances. But those hard-earned anecdotes and life lessons I'd learned firsthand still came in handy during those late-night phone calls; it seems the great equalizer—regardless of the situation—is that we can all make it through with a little help from our friends. And the fact that Jennifer and I went through it together made it all that much easier to be there for our friend when she needed us the most.

We'd lived it, breathed it, laughed, and cried through it. Sometimes it was unbearable. Like on my first Christmas as a single gal, when I couldn't bear the thought of sending out Christmas cards because it would be tangible proof, certified by the United States Postal system, that my family no longer included my husband. Other times it . . . well, okay, the thing you need to realize, is that most of the first year was pretty unbearable. And even if you've set up your own personal war room with white boards, Post-Its, and computerized Gantt charts, at some point things won't go as planned, and you'll end up learning the hard way. Like when I decided to take in a movie on Valentine's Day, only to discover that, while I'd avoided all of the amorous adults out for a romantic dinner, I was surrounded by teenagers and the newly acquired knowledge that young couples who want to get to third base go to dark places that serve popcorn in buckets.

And even if the year ahead as a soon-to-be-single woman starts to resemble Mr. Toad's Wild Ride (albeit without the long lines and warning to keep your hands inside the car), this book's mission is simple, its goal attainable. I want to give you the lay of the land, help you process what's happening, and discover that this isn't the end of the world. It's just your entrée into a slightly different world than the one you were used to.

As you face this big challenge, there will be times when you may be thinking that this is one situation where you have no choice but to fly by the seat of your pants. Wrong, divorcing girlfriend; I'd beg to differ. There are instances where a few well-chosen Dos and Don'ts can provide some much-needed guidance. Because benefiting from the experience of others is a big, giant Do, you can look to these pithy examples in each chapter of good and not-so-good ways to react to the situation at hand. Thinking you have to learn things the hard way, well, that'd be a Don't. There's a reason people are always saying there's no need to reinvent the wheel, and in this case, there's no need to suffer through the bad decisions when other women have blazed the trail before you.

Rest assured, you have friends on the other side. And by other side, I don't mean dead restless souls in between worlds, psychic visions, and Ouija boards. No, this other side is life after your marriage has ended. Life as an independent unit. One. You. Single. Are you reading this book curled up in bed? Snuggled on your couch? Hidden away from others because you are about to enter the precarious world of the formerly married, to become an ex, and venture out into the harsh reality of a table for one? That's okay. For now. Things will change, though; time has a way of ensuring that. Maybe by the last chapter you'll be reading this on the commuter train, or on the no. 6 express bus, not the least bit concerned about what the rest of the world is wondering about the girl sans wedding ring. Maybe, eventually, the term *unmarried* won't cause the nervous twitch over your right eye. You'll throw caution to the wind and go out for a night on the town—alone. And maybe you'll be surprised by how many others are out there just like you—members of the Divorced Girls' Society who have realized that their newly acquired single status isn't a life sentence, but merely one of life's many unexpected changes.

Initiation:
The First Twenty-Four Hours

I discovered my marriage was over while strad-dling a Samsonite. There I was, agonizing over which bikini to bring to Ipanema, and it ends up my husband was agonizing over how to tell me that he didn't want to be married anymore. *Oh, and by the way, the trip to Brazil's been cancelled.*

Regardless of who's making their declaration of independence, the first twenty-four hours after the announcement are trying ones, fraught with anger, resentment, fear, sadness, and about a bil-lion other emotions fighting for airtime. Each swipe of the second hand can feel like an eternity, and all of a sudden you're facing eternity alone.

In my case, there was an immediate spiraling, internal dialogue that repeated itself over and over like a song you can't get out of your head. It sounded something like this:

1. This can't be happening.
2. Surely, he isn't serious.
3. How long has he felt this way?
4. How could I not know?
5. Therapy! Counseling! We shall overcome!
6. Return to number one and start all over again.

Of course, it really *was* happening, he *was* serious, I had *no idea* how long the words had been perched on his lips, and I had to be a completely oblivious moron with all of the intuition of an oak tree not to know it. Still, no matter how many times I repeated steps one through six of that useless dialog, it didn't change the fact that my marriage was over. And that's when the new voices kicked in. And they sounded a little like that short, round woman in *Poltergeist*.

Ignore the Voices in Your Head—Haven't You Ever Seen a Stephen King Movie?

Your head is not in the best place to be making decisions right now—at least not any *good* decisions. This is why it's not so much what you must *do* within the first twenty-four hours, as what you must *stop yourself from doing*. In the mood to rent *War of the Roses*? Hide the Blockbuster card. Feel like a Kathy Bates flick? Perhaps *Misery* isn't your best choice. Googling the lasting effects of tightie-whities on male fertility? Step away from the computer and pick up a book (preferably not the unauthorized biography of Lizzie Borden).

The point is, whatever pops into your head, don't act on it. Why? Because while it might feel really good, it could end up hurting you later: in court, with your settlement, with custody issues. That little emotional drama bit could unfairly peg you as the fruitcake, and that won't get you far when you're trying to build a case in your favor. So, none of this tossing his clothes out the second-story window, slashing the steel-belted radials he relies on to get to work, and certainly no calling the IRS on that one commission check he never claimed on his taxes back in 1994. You are as good as crazy right now. Understand that and let the crazed bitch rest. Calm her with a bucket of Betty Crocker chocolate frosting and sugar cookies for dipping. Or a trip to Saks. She needs to be distracted. Later, you can redirect that energy toward more positive initiatives that help you move through the process. But now is not the time to indulge her.

The Divorced Girls' Society
TOOLKIT

The Purge Page

Don't keep those nefarious plans bottled up. While we don't believe that now is the best time to act on your urge to snip your soon-to-be ex-husband's face out of every family photo, we don't think you need to let those thoughts take up much-needed mental real estate, either. So here's your opportunity to get them out, to purge yourself of these thoughts so you can free up your head for more productive activities. Write down every outrageous, bitchy, inappropriate thought you're having. Then take a deep breath and move on.

1. _____

2. _____

3. _____

4. _____

5. _____

More than five thoughts? Aren't you prolific! Get yourself a piece of paper and keep on going. Better you get them out now than end up writing them on a yellow legal pad in the interrogation room of the city jail while being watched through two-way glass later.

Kiss the Old You Goodbye!

That woman who could take a conference call, bathe a kid, fold the laundry, and plan next week's meals without getting even a splash of Mr. Bubble on her freshly pressed shirt? She's still you. Unfortunately, while the super abilities that enabled you to paint your toes with one hand while cleaning out the fridge with the other still exist, the rational you will be tossed aside like last year's linen espadrilles with the long ankle ribbons. When something as big as the end of your marriage is facing you, it can affect you in so many unexpected ways. "Unexpected" is the key term here, which is why you need to lay low, not react, plan, or plot. Accept that and promise yourself you won't actually do anything other than tell your closest family and friends. That's all you need to do. Even if it's just to tell one person. You must tell . . . someone. No other activity should take place. No matter how sane and reasonable an idea may seem.

Hour One

You've heard the expression, "after the shock wears off"? Well, that doesn't happen here. You'll be in shock for a while. And you need comforting right now. Don't try to handle this alone. Get to a friend (sisters and moms count, too). You'll need to recount the scene that seems to be in a continuous mental loop in your head—regardless of who made the announcement. Talking it out immediately, sharing the play-by-play, isn't simply a way to extend the torture and involve others in your misery. It actually serves several purposes other than depleting your body of excess tears and ensuring bloodshot eyes. To wit:

1. Telling a few close people means you can't hide. Sure, instead of talking to a friend you could crawl into bed, pull the comforter up tight, and hope you awake to discover it was all a bad dream, but that only worked for J. R. Ewing. So unless you're the star of your own highly rated TV show, simply rubbing the vanilla-scented bath gel out of your eyes isn't going to make this go away.

2. It makes you say the words out loud, puts them out there into the universe where you can't pretend it's not happening. Sure, you'll be retelling the story through fits and starts, through choking, gasping sniffles, but it's out there and now you own it. And we all know that ownership is nine-tenths of the law. So it must mean something.

3. It reminds you that, while your spouse will no longer be enjoying the pleasure of your company, there are other people out there who love you, runny nose and all.

What Your GIRLFRIEND *Is Thinking*

Your friend calls you with the news. It's something big. Maybe a promotion (she is terribly intelligent, after all). Or a baby (yea! a trip to Baby Gap). Maybe even the winning lottery numbers (of course, then you'd have to hate her, unless she splurges for a great all-girls trip to the Caribbean).

No, it's her marriage. It's over. "No way," I gasped, realizing too late that I sounded very much like a sixteen-year-old who just found out her best friend's boyfriend broke up with her, and very little like a grownup who wants to be there for her friend. And that's when it occurred to me: I had no idea how to respond to the news that my best friend's life just irrevocably changed forever.

There's a rush of reactions swirling around in your head when your friend calls to drop the bomb: disbelief (surely this is just a bump in the road), concern (will she ever get out of bed again?), and anger (the prick); the 101 questions you ask her twelve different ways (when? where were you? what did he say, exactly?); your desire to rescue her and make it all better (I'll be on the first flight out); and, finally, the realization that no matter what you do, her life is coming apart.

Within the first few hours of the announcement, and well into the next several days, the event played nonstop in my mind, completely and without pause, the same way an annoying song enters your brain, and for reasons that defy you, you somehow know all of the words, and you keep singing it, even though you keep telling yourself, "I hate that song! I hate that song!" It went like this: the strange look on my husband's face, the sinking feeling that overcame me, the fear that something bad was about to happen. I had asked, "What's wrong with you?" and expected him to admit to jet lag (he had come in from L.A. the night before), a pain in a part of his body (his hypochondria was legendary), or some news about his family (was his flaky brother coming to live with us again, for the third time in ten years?). But it was his deadpan voice, the way he looked at me like I was a foreign object, as if he couldn't quite make out the strange woman standing with a suitcase between her legs, a Coppertone bottle in her hand, that told me it had to do with us. And it was bad.

MANTRAS **to get you through the day**

Help is not a four-letter word.

When he said, "I don't want to be married anymore," inside I screamed, "What?!" But on the outside, I simply stared. I pride myself on the ability to remain unruffled when everything and everyone is ruffling. I held it together. I was good. In my calmest voice I replied, "I'll give you one week to think about what you want to do. I think we need to see a counselor. If you don't want to, then you need to tell me what your plans are. And you'll need to find somewhere else to sleep." I was actually thinking of his friend Bill's house when I said that, but he interpreted "somewhere else" as our third-floor guest room. It didn't hurt that the third floor housed the pool table he just *had* to get, or that we had a microwave and beer fridge up there as well. The man was no dummy.

But neither was I. I took those old Dry Idea commercials to heart—I never let him see me sweat. On the outside, I was a rock. Inside, I was in shock.

Tips for Your SPEED-DIAL SISTERS

As tempting as it may be, do not:

1. Ask too many questions in an effort to try and figure out what went wrong. It went wrong, and that's all you need to know for now.
2. Remind the divorcing gal of every time she voiced her own dissatisfaction with the soon-to-be ex-spouse in the hope that it will make her feel better. It won't. (Example: Do not remind her that she once told you he was bad in bed, his morning breath could start a forest fire, or that she couldn't stand his crazy mother.)
3. Tell her every detestable trait her husband embodied, or remind her that you always said he was a jerk. It doesn't help, and you'll only sound like an I-told-you-so.

Welcome to the World of It-Could-Never-Happen-to-Me

How could this happen to me? What did I do to deserve this? I had the cute kid, the nice job, the whole Brady-Bunch thing going on (without the other five kids), the Jack-and-Jill bathroom, and a housekeeper named Alice. It seriously never dawned on me that it would ever end. How could it? I was the daughter that my mother-in-law never had. We bought a vacation home six months before. He just upgraded my ring in May! Welcome to the world of it-could-never-happen-to-me. Also known as Delusionville. Come on in and get comfortable; you may be here a while.

Columbo Looked Good in Khaki— Why Shouldn't I?

It's terribly tempting at this point to attempt to figure out *why*. Why is this happening? Why couldn't I fix it? Why now? If you're the one deciding to leave, you're probably asking yourself why you just couldn't force yourself to be happy. If you're the one being left, you're probably wondering what you did wrong. At the end of the day, it doesn't change anything. Even if you could pinpoint the exact moment your marriage ceased to live up to its promises, it doesn't matter. Perhaps you believe that playing Columbo—that identifying the date and time of the crime—will give you a sense of control and understanding. But if you are hankering to solve a mystery, pick up Agatha Christie. Leave the postmortem of your marriage alone . . . for now.

Hour Two

My first two hours were surreal. I left my house as soon as I could, and chose a place I felt I could be anonymous: an outdoor mall. I sat on a bench between Restoration Hardware and April Cornell, and made all of the requisite calls: mom, dad, sis, and Jennifer. All were in utter disbelief—which, in hindsight, was helpful. If someone had barked, "Well, yeah, I've been waiting for him to

pull this on you . . . you had to see this coming, right?"
I think I might have dissolved right there next to Restoration Hardware's sign for its Famous Fall Lighting Sale. If this is, indeed, the response you received upon declaring the news, this is probably a good time to begin learning about the Get-Out-of-Jail-Free Card (page 12). But in my case, the family and best friend responded appropriately.

My dad, ever the optimist, insisted that my husband probably needed a few months away from me, and that he'd snap out of it. "*It* being *what*?" I'd wanted to ask. A seething desire to be away from me? In any case, as much as I felt like that wouldn't happen, my dad's hope gave me hope. Each time I retold the story (four times in total, and each time a little different depending upon the audience), it got easier. I wanted my family to think I had my act together, that I was being strong. I didn't need to, though. I should have realized that it's normal to break down, to feel like you've stepped onto the Free Fall ride at Six Flags and forgotten to buckle the belt tightly across your lap.

The Divorced Girls' Society
GOLDEN RULES

- Do stick close to friends who are not emotionally needy and can handle your occasional manic behavior.
- Do stay away from things that you think will send your emotions into a tornado-like spiral—e.g., giving a reading at your niece's wedding, the seafood restaurant where he proposed, the photo album of your trip to Seattle.

- Do let your emotions get out; remember, it's normal to be feeling a lot these days. The caveat here is: You don't want to hyperventilate, gasp, and choke your way through a meeting with your boss, so self-control is sometimes necessary. But if you're driving to work and that song comes on, it's okay to let it out there. Just check your mascara before you get out of the car.
- Don't pick up other bad habits in an effort to stifle what you're feeling. This is not the time to stop eating regularly or to mix a batch of bloody marys for the insulated commuter cup on your drive in to work.
- Don't spend time thinking about how other people perceive your apparent inability to control your emotions.
- Don't forget to be good to yourself. Calling in sick one day could come in handy. As could a manicure, or a trip to the department store for some new lipstick.

Looking Out for Number One

Looking out for number one does not translate to "Be a shitty person," "Take out your sadness and frustration on well-meaning friends and family members," or "Bitch out the girl at the drycleaners when she asks if you want medium starch." It simply means keep the focus on you. Your emotional needs trump all others' right now, for no other reason than you are in a psychologically precarious spot these days. You know that because you burst into tears watching the Channel 6 weather report, or when the postman waves as he drives by. Did you promise to help your neighbor pick out new drapes for her family room? Perhaps now isn't the best time to be making decisions that involve plaid versus polka dots—after all, lately, selecting which pair of socks to wear sends you into convulsive sobs. Was your sister expecting you to take her puppy to obedience school on Tuesday afternoons from three to four? A housebroken puppy is now the least of your problems. A lot of the stuff you're experiencing is hitting you with the force of a linebacker, with no warning whatsoever. So, do everyone a favor and pay attention to your feelings over all others'.

The Get-Out-of-Jail-Free Card

It may sound selfish and self-indulgent, but really, you have earned it. It's part of your emotional-management strategy. You are allowed to act in ways that fly in the face of all of the social norms and niceties your mom drilled into you as a child: interrupting people, cutting short a social situation that makes you uncomfortable, asking someone to stop talking about a subject matter that bothers you. It's all allowed, *for now*. Think of it as a get-out-of-jail-free card, which you get to carry for about a year. Whip it out as needed. Know that, for the most part, people will understand. If they don't understand, that's okay; you may want to put those friends and family members on the back burner while you go through this. You have yourself to take care of, and you can't be managing other egos and personalities during this very critical time. It doesn't minimize other crises, because bad things happen to all of us. Obviously, if you have a friend who is going through something equally traumatic, then your perceived self-absorbed behavior may not be her antidote, even though it's yours. Generally speaking, you'd do best to steer clear of those people who cannot temporarily adjust to your crisis. You are in no position to negotiate or bargain for emotional support and understanding, or to ask for forgiveness when you may not be displaying the most ladylike behavior. You need to be candid and straightforward with your friends and family; tell them what you need—and more importantly what you don't need—right now.

What Your GIRLFRIEND Is Thinking

I met Vicki's soon-to-be ex-husband about three weeks after they started dating. So when she told me about her pending divorce, I had fourteen years of memories to sift through to try and understand why he wanted out. I mean, there had to be a reason, right? I started remembering every conversation, every little hint he may have dropped along the way: when he told me his friends never thought he'd ever get married; how he thought he was too selfish to have children; his adamant insistence that any woman he married would take his last name. And I wasn't the only one playing amateur sleuth. When I talked to mutual friends, they'd inevitably be trying to figure out the very same thing. "Was there another woman?" was usually the first question. And the second, without exception, "Is he gay?" The first time I heard this, I laughed (okay, and the second and third time, too). And then I realized there was more to this question than the perverse wish that we could blame Vicki's situation on her husband's misguided decision to get married in the first place. We needed to find an explanation, no matter how absurd and out there it may be, because we needed to make sense out of a nonsensical situation.

The Divorced Girls' Society
TOOLKIT

When to Use Your Get-Out-of-Jail-Free Cards

- A friend invites you to the movies, where a romantic scene between lovers hits you right where you live. Use your card to get up and leave right then and there. Tell your friend you'll meet her later or ask her to call you when she gets home.

- You've committed to baking 3,000 chocolate chip cookies for the PTA fundraiser next month. No, you can't bail out on 3,000 cookies, much as you'd like to. Instead, use your card to offer to bake 300, and say you'll find other volunteers to take care of the other 2,700 (yeah, good luck with that).

- Your friend wants to have dinner at her favorite restaurant—which also happens to be the spot where you celebrated your 10th anniversary. Out comes the card. Suggest another spot or recommend she find another companion that night. You can always do dinner somewhere else next Saturday.

DIVORCED GIRLS' SOCIETY TENETS

✓ The first twenty-four hours of the announcement of your divorce—no matter who announced it—are mind-numbing; accept that and don't do anything hasty.

✓ Trying to figure out why this is happening will not change the fact that it is happening, and that means you need to stop thinking about him and start thinking about you.

✓ Tell someone close to you so you can begin processing what's going on, and we don't mean the woman behind the counter at Target.

✓ Surrounding yourself with supportive people and looking out for number one is not selfish and self-indulgent; it's an emotional-management strategy that can help get you through what's ahead.

Allies, War Generals, and Freeze-Dried Hungarian Goulash

While the sudden bursts of gasping sobs still came frequently and at the most inopportune moments (deli line at Kroger, weekly status meeting on value-proposition strategies), life was moving on and I had work to do! The key now was to rally my allies and begin developing my strategy. I was at war. War as in enemies, allies, bunkers, and freeze-dried Hungarian goulash. This approach may seem extreme and unnecessary (especially the goulash), but preparing for the worst-case scenario is crucial to success here. For all intents and purposes, you're about to engage in a war; whether it's a harmless pillow fight or full scale, atomic-style nuclear annihilation is actually not important now. It may be easier to psyche yourself up for a full-on North

Korea-like conflict, and then allow yourself to be totally surprised (and delighted) when the opposing side suggests a mild game of Parcheesi instead.

"We aren't at war with each other," you insist, "we're simply parting company, separating amicably." Yeah. Spare me, sister. Look, the fact is, when a formerly lovey-dovey couple starts talking about who gets what, and money becomes the primary subject matter, things can't help but get ugly. Cindy Lauper had it right— money changes everything, and sometimes it brings out the worst in us. Now, maybe you won't fall prey to this unfortunate reality. But maybe *he* will. Taking a pre-emptive approach will prepare you no matter how the other side reacts.

Uncle Sam May Want You, But I Need You: Recruiting Your Allies

Now it was time to recruit. I needed experts, advisors, people who knew about this messy divorce stuff and who could help me get through it with my finances, and what little sanity I had left, still intact. I decided that the two most valuable players on my team would be my therapist and my attorney. And I had to find good ones. Fast.

Therapists? Lawyers? Sounds so *Melrose Place*, doesn't it? Only this isn't make-believe, and chances are there isn't a leggy blonde next door who, between walking around the community pool in a string bikini and hanging her intimates over the stair banister, also just happens to be a Harvard Law School graduate with killer courtroom instincts. How to find the good therapists and attorneys, that's the challenge.

Finding the Right Attorney for You

I know this probably goes without saying, but I feel it needs to be said. Please promise that no matter what, you will not call any attorney who:

1. Has purchased a full-size ad on the back cover of the yellow pages, or
2. Has a television ad campaign complete with a promise that "we don't get paid unless you win," coupled with a catchy jingle that includes his phone number. Rule number two happens to dovetail nicely into rule number three:
3. Has a phone number that spells out something like 1-800-I-M-VICTIM—your ally here needs to, plain and simple, understand the divorce business.

We're not suggesting that these attorneys are less than reputable, or that a desire to see one's face on a billboard overlooking I-95 isn't perfectly normal in an era of celebrity trials, but this is *divorce*, people! No, it's more important than that—it's *your* divorce. You want someone you can trust 100 percent. You need someone you feel comfortable talking to about some very uncomfortable topics. Whoever you end up choosing will be in your life at least until the papers are signed, sealed, and delivered. Divorce is a very personal process, and choosing the right person to represent you throughout the process can go a long way toward making it less painful. How much consideration did you put into selecting a dry cleaner, a hairdresser, or a kennel for Mr. Whiskers? You can live without that silk shirt with the pizza-sauce stain, your hair will always grow back, and Mr. Whiskers doesn't *really* need a cashmere scratching post; but you need a divorce attorney who's on your side, so take your time and choose wisely.

Lawyer Jokes Exist for a Reason

Sure, family lawyers are great. They know what they're doing. They use big words that make you feel all warm and fuzzy, things like "primary interrogatories" and "habeus corpus." They make you feel taken care of, but that fuzzy feeling comes with a price tag that can be hard to swallow. And if you and your spouse have decided this won't be a knock-down, drag-out battle, perhaps there's a better option for you. Enter the mediator.

A mediator is a neutral third party who helps to negotiate an agreement between you and your spouse. They can help resolve key issues, including visitation, child support, custody, alimony, and property division. During the mediation sessions, you may still have an attorney or financial planner present, and at the end of the process the mediator creates a settlement agreement for your divorce. My friend used a mediator with great success, so don't discard this option simply because it seems less "official." It all depends on your situation. And, sometimes, your wallet.

Beyond understanding family law, your legal ally should be someone with experience. She will protect you from what's bad about divorce law, and make the most out of what's good. Personal rapport also plays a part here. You don't want to feel intimidated by your attorney; you are, after all, the one signing the checks. The time you spend in the cushy offices of Read, Uhm,

& Weep will conjure up all sorts of emotions. You need to be comfortable asking for a box of tissues one minute and discussing finances the next. Your lawyer doesn't need to be your best friend—in fact, that would be one very costly friendship—but there has to be a basic level of trust and ease in your interactions.

Think of your attorney as your strategic planner, your own personal Norman Schwartzkopf, only she doesn't require that you salute—at least not if your check clears. I found my lawyer through my alumnae club; there are lots of ways to get recommendations—here's where knowing how to play the legal field's version of Six Degrees of Kevin Bacon can really pay off.

The Divorced Girls' Society
TOOLKIT

Where to Find an Attorney That's Your Perfect Fit

- **Friends.** Maybe you have a friend who's been down the divorce road before you and would love to share her attorney's name, phone number, and personal e-mail. But even if your friends don't know a legal brief from a Hanes brief, chances are they know somebody who does. A brother who made the parents proud by making law review? A cousin who worked as a paralegal after college? They can all help steer you in the right direction.
- **Attorneys in other states.** There are networks that keep all attorneys connected, so chances are even if your only legal connection happens to be a twelve-

hour ride away, he or she may be able to direct you to somebody in your hometown.

- **Alumnae organizations.** Most colleges maintain databases that allow you to search by occupation. While you may not want to hire somebody who burned her bra over a homecoming bonfire, she may just be managing partner in a law firm with the best divorce attorneys this side of an underwire.
- **American Bar Association.** The American Bar Association has an online referral service that can be helpful if you really don't know where to start. Because there are state and local chapters, you can ask for referrals to local attorneys with the expertise you need—and the referrals are free! Got to *www.abanet.org* and click on "lawyer locator."

Finally, and I cannot stress this one piece of advice enough: If you choose to go the lawyer route, get your own. Do not share an attorney. Don't do it. Remember, this is war, and warring parties don't share a general, ammunition, or foxholes. A shared attorney can't have both of your best interests in mind, unless you and your ex see eye to eye on everything. Did that happen when you were happily married? If not, how can that happen now that you're unhappily parting?

No, this will not be fun—this isn't Hollywood's version of divorce with the hot attorney asking you out as soon as the judgment is handed down. Yes, you will probably grow to hate every interaction with your lawyer. But you need one to ensure you are financially and legally protected. And as much as you think you might be a smarty pants about many subjects, unless you are a lawyer, trust me when I say that there's a bunch of stuff you don't know about the law, marriage dissolution, divided assets, and custody. And this isn't the time to find out what you don't know.

Keep a Pen Handy

Your lawyer's effectiveness is in large part dependent upon the information you provide her. She's only going to know what you tell her, and because this is lawyerly stuff, she's going to want to see proof. So you can go on and on about your ex's big 401(k), but you also need to get your hands on the documents. Lawyers work with evidence, and you are the keeper of said evidence, so prepare yourself for hours and hours culling through old check statements, credit card account balances, and various other financial documentation. It will be harsh, it will suck at times, but getting this information together will go a long way in ensuring that you come out on top.

Which is why now is a good time to recommend that you start keeping track of *everything*. In military speak, it's about surveillance and reconnaissance. It doesn't matter who initiated the situation, or how fine either of you are with the impending dissolution of your marriage. People do crazy things in times of emotional uncertainty, and during this time of in-between existences (in between being married and being single), you'll want to take good notes, maintain an attention to detail, and keep a close eye out. Why? Because you can't know what is going through your ex's head right now. And sometimes people act out in strange ways. You want to make sure it's not with your assets or bank account.

Strange behavior, unusual spending habits—any kind of change—need to be noted by you. This is not about catching him in the act of anything illegal or immoral. You're not doing this for any specific reason right now—this isn't intended to be your big Kojak moment, when you relish the chance to surprise your spouse with carefully collected information ("A-ha! I knew you had a gerbil fetish—what's with the $750 expenditures at Pets R Us?!"). This data is for you and your attorney to determine how best to leverage. You are simply keeping thorough notes on the goings-on as the two of you move through this process. If, for example, you start to notice that an automatic withdrawal is taking place from your joint checking account, so it's going out but you've no clue as to what account it's being transferred to, that's noteworthy. And as crass as this sounds, the financial part of it can become ugly, so better to have things documented and recorded and keep it official and nonemotional. Keep closer tabs on your checking account statements, credit card statements, and any other records of joint spending and cash flow. And if something seems out of place or questionable, go with your gut, and share the information with your attorney.

Even though, in your eyes, this may be a vanilla-flavored divorce, who's to say it won't change to something more complicated in the future (bye-bye, vanilla—hello, caramel swirl with coffee-chocolate chunks). Remember, for most, divorce is a drawn-out process (unless you're a Hollywood starlet, in which case, you can get married on Monday, divorced on Tuesday, and be back to videotaping sex scenes with an aging big-hair-band rocker on Thursday). You'll need to keep track of what's going on in the six to twelve months preceding the actual divorce trial.

As much as I felt like a sorry excuse for Lois Lane, with pencil perched behind my left ear, notebook in hand, as I diligently logged all happenings in my day-to-day life, I did it. Things like logging those nights my ex came home late, while I arrived home at 5:30 on the nose each night, were just the proof I needed to tell a compelling story that demonstrated that I was, indeed, my daughter's primary caregiver. I'm not going to lie to you: It felt petty at times. It felt like something out of a bad Lifetime Television movie, only instead of Meredith Baxter Birney's blonde tresses, it was my own mousy brown hair shaking from side to side as I cursed myself for being so calculated, paranoid, or classically soon-to-be-ex-wife-y. It never even occurred to me that I would actually need that information at my trial. Or that it would come in so handy.

This isn't paranoia. This is you being proactive. This is you being smart.

You may never need the information you end up collecting, but better safe than sorry. I kept track of my ex's apartment expenditures ($2500 on new furniture to furnish an apartment that I did not agree to)—and I was reimbursed for it at my trial. There are so many little details, so many things that you may not even be paying attention to, that it's best to simply buy yourself a lovely writing utensil, treat yourself to one of those cloth-covered journals that always seemed so impractical before, and write it all down. Just don't forget to let your attorney know so, together, you can use the information as needed.

What Your GIRLFRIEND *Is Thinking*

After Vicki's big announcement, the idea of putting a bikini in my suitcase started to sound scary, and not just because I hadn't hit the gym in ages. All she'd done was pack for a trip to Brazil—a trip I was envious of because it would include sand, sun, and rounds of Caipirinha cocktails while I was home packing lunch boxes with ham sandwiches—and the next thing she knew, it was splitsville. Poof, her marriage up in smoke, faster than you can say Gisele Bundchen.

I can honestly say that I never expected to get Vicki's call. When my husband and I would speculate about which of our friends were most likely to fall into the 50 percent that gets divorced, Vicki never ended up in the group of have-nots. I always thought Vicki was an ideal wife, a great mother, a perfect partner. In fact, she was way better at the marriage thing than I ever was.

After the shock wore off and I had time to come to grips with the idea of my best friend's divorce, I couldn't help but admit what should have been obvious from the beginning: If it could happen to her, it could happen to me.

I'm Listening . . .

Therapists are like friends without opinions. You know how you have friends who are great listeners, the ones who are always there for you? A therapist is like that, except you pay her for that. Okay, you pay her for more than that. You pay her to help you manage the emotions that are churning inside you like a day-old burrito. She validates what you're feeling, and she helps you process your emotions in more productive ways. So when you have fantasies about your ex pulling a Sonny Bono on the slopes of Aspen, or when you listen eagerly for traffic reports that include bad pile-ups on the highways he takes to work every day, your therapist can redirect, or confirm, your current emotional navigation pattern. Are you twisted and demented? Perhaps, but it may only be temporary.

At first consideration, the idea of talking to a complete stranger (albeit with credentials) may seem odd or even questionably helpful. After all, how can this person—who you have to make an appointment with, who will peer at you over her glasses and make mysterious notes on her pad—make getting through your divorce any easier? She can help because she knows the clinical reasons for why you are feeling like Sybil, or why you want to smash you-know-who's face through a plate-glass window. You can say whatever you want to your therapist and not worry about her judging you, like, say, your mom or opinionated friend might.

A first visit to a therapist's office should not be a hand-wringing one. This person is on your side. Keep that in mind, and remove all concerns of "What is she thinking?" Also remember that you are not the first woman to be going through this, and chances are, your therapist has heard your story before. As with your attorney, your therapist is only as helpful as the information you provide. She's there to sort through all of the messages, feelings, and thoughts going on inside your head, so the more you get out, the more helpful she can be. Don't be shy, and don't hold back. I actually told my therapist that I secretly fantasized about my ex getting hurt—I mean really hurt—so specifically that I had the event all planned out in my head. Did my therapist dial 911 and rat me out because I was *thisclose* to attempting homicide? No. She listened, and then explained to me that the anger I was feeling was completely normal. In fact, she went on, that if I wasn't feeling anything, then wouldn't that suggest that I had been in an emotionless marriage? The lack of feeling is more alarming than the psychotic, chainsaw massacre I had planned out in my head, my therapist assured me.

Don't try to out-analyze your analyst. At my first meeting, my therapist asked me if I wanted something to drink. I fretted over that decision, concerned that a request for tea might have me pegged as spineless, coffee would mean I was aggressive, and water could reveal my frugal qualities. The truth was, she wasn't trying to look for the deep-seated meaning behind my drink of choice; she was simply being polite. You're not there to analyze her; you're there to feel better. Focus on that, and your sessions will help you.

So let it all out—that's what she's there for. You can even cry for the full session, too, if you wish. It's your time (remember, you're paying her). And don't worry, she will always have a box of tissues nearby.

Choosing a Therapist

As with recruiting your attorney, there are some reliable sources you can use to find a therapist that meets your needs. Check with your health-care provider first to see what kinds of mental-health coverage you qualify for. (And don't let the term "mental health" throw you—it's a commonplace term and does not in any way suggest that you are on your way to lobotomy-town.) Your health-care provider can give you a list of mental-health experts in your area. They will also be categorized by specialty—family therapy, child therapy, eating disorders—the list goes on. You can count on having a pretty large selection of mental-health experts to choose from in the family-therapy specialty; it's a pretty popular field.

You can also ask around. A friend of mine told me she was seeing a therapist, and she seemed satisfied with her progress and the therapist's style. I checked her out, and that therapist actually recommended another one who ended up being the one I use today. See how the network can work in mysterious ways?

Therapists have different ways of interacting with their patients, so this is an area that becomes pretty subjective when you're choosing. I would recommend meeting with a few and then determining which one you feel most comfortable opening up to. Be sure to consider all parts of the interaction: How does she react? Are you comfortable talking to her? Does she talk too much? Too little? Just right? Here are a few other things to consider:

A man or a woman? While at first it might seem natural to gravitate toward a woman, the sex of your therapist isn't really important unless it really matters to you. A woman won't necessarily understand you better. She won't necessarily be a better listener or offer better counsel. She may have a prettier office, but you're not there to admire the décor; you're there to partake in some professional help.

Location, location, location. That therapist your best friend used when she was getting divorced? The one that's thirty miles away down a dirt road that isn't plowed in the winter? Maybe not the best choice. No matter how much you like a therapist, no matter how highly recommended, it won't do you any good if you can't find the time to go because a fifty-minute session requires a half-hour ferry ride and three-mile trek on the back of a donkey. In order to really be of value, visiting your therapist should be as convenient as stopping for that ice-cream cone after work every Friday.

High on the comfort level, low on the stress. There has to be a comfort level between you and your therapist, because you're going to be disclosing everything. Talking finances and child custody with your attorney will seem like an hour-long massage (with aromatherapy) compared to the fifty minutes you'll spend at your therapist's office. This is your opportunity to let it all out, to indulge the voices that keep you up at night. And that requires complete and total honesty—with yourself. Can you really focus on how you're feeling when all you can do is stare at the distorted neon artwork on the wall? Does the idea of being forced to lie down on a white leather couch with brass rivets make you uneasy? Will you really be able to open up to a person who insists you call her Sister Goddess Ophelia? If not, it's time to find a different therapist. Maybe an office with scenes from *The Hobbit* painted on the ceiling is the right environment for some people. But if it's not right for you, move on. You are what this is all about.

Credentials. Sure, diplomas are impressive, but when it comes to choosing the right therapist to work with, do you really need Sigmund Freud? Luckily, there are plenty of professionals to choose from when it comes to therapy. Maybe you'd prefer to speak with someone who knows you and who shares your family's history, like the clergy at your church. Or maybe your wallet would prefer you speak with a mental-health counselor who has the training you're after, but a price tag you can swallow. There are psychologists with Ph.D.s, psychiatrists with M.D.s, counselors with M.A.s, and licensed social workers. Don't discount someone because they lack the "right" diplomas or degrees. Do choose someone because you trust them and feel you can develop a rapport.

Closing Ranks

With my attorney and therapist firmly on my side, I made my first pre-emptive decision: I made my ex's family off limits. No talking, no interacting, not even an e-mail. No matter how great a pal I was with his mom, no matter that we shared the same taste in nail polish and sad movies, she was only going to get caught in the crossfire. She would always be my daughter's grandmother, my ex-mother-in-law, and a part of my life, but right now I had to draw a line in the sand, and she was firmly entrenched on his side. How could she not be? Isn't every mother on their child's side? Even the lunatic axe murderer has his mom on his side. Even though my mother-in-law and I had been friends, I knew which side she'd be aligned with—I accepted that, and then planned around it. As much as I hated not having her with me, she wasn't even eligible for the draft. I considered her flat footed and moved on.

My friends, the people I brought into the relationship, I have to admit, I didn't for a second assume would continue to communicate with my ex after the announcement. It wasn't as if they called him every week to revisit the latest episode of *Grey's Anatomy*. When it came right down to it, the friendships we'd forged over the years could be grouped into three camps—mine, his, and ours. The "ours" were really the only place it could get sticky. And if you're someone who, while married, developed friendships with people you shared equally—say the couple you met in Lamaze class—then you may want to decide how to handle these relationships jointly. These people may decide to avoid the draft, become conscientious objectors, and that's fine. In any case, it's time to decide who is truly your ally, because in the coming months you'll need comrades in arms—and it's nice to know up front who'll be marching by your side.

It's completely understandable that some of the friends you formerly shared will now be firmly ensconced in the enemy's camp. Sure, you may have thought you and your ex's best friend had a great connection—you both recognized and publicly made fun of the way your ex-husband would tug on his lower lip when he was nervous. You and he both loved an amaretto on ice, and you secretly thought he was cute and enjoyed hanging out with him. But the fact remains that your ex's best friend started—and will remain—in your ex's army. The good news is, you've plenty of A-players in your army, so let him have what's rightfully his.

If you need to—if you think it will help—don't hesitate to make yourself a list of friends you know you can count on, as well as those who fall into both camps. Then turn to your Toolkit on the next page.

The Divorced Girls' Society
TOOLKIT

Your Battalion

List friends and acquaintances and the roles you'd like them to play during the upcoming months—or the roles you think they'll end up fulfilling. Knowing ahead of time what you can expect, and from whom, will help you get the lay of the land—and share your night-vision goggles.

Mine*	His	Ours
_____	_____	_____
_____	_____	_____
_____	_____	_____
_____	_____	_____
_____	_____	_____

*Make special note of which of *your* allies will become Speed-Dial Sisters—friendship's version of the Special Forces. These friends will be called upon to serve in extreme conditions and should be up to the task. Better yet, they're prepared to take up arms and fight by your side.

Living with the Insurgent

Sometimes it's not possible to make a clean break right away, and you're forced to live with the very person you'd just as soon avoid. When living with the insurgent under these conditions, awkward moments become more frequent as you move from married couple into sort-of-single-but-not-really and finally into really single. One of the first and stickiest problems you'll have to deal with while embarking on your sort-of-single-but-not-really status will be the rules around how to cohabitate. And, as if that weren't troublesome enough, it can be made worse by the existence of little ones in the household, tykes who you'll want to shield from the awkwardness. The giant elephant in the room (or, to be more specific, in the family room, when you want to watch your favorite show, and the giant elephant is lounging quite comfortably across all three couch cushions) is: determining and agreeing upon the rules for sharing the house while you both have to be there. As tempting as it may be, don't go the passive-aggressive route. Don't make coffee in the morning, but only enough for you. Or, make his favorite meal and conspicuously set the table only for you and your children. Remember, maturity counts. Save that mental energy and conspiring for more rewarding endeavors.

Begin by identifying what's important to you, and ask or negotiate for it. If you want the TV on Wednesday nights, say that. Treat the relationship as if you were two roommates, nothing more. Use that as the filter for how to communicate. So while you want to say, "I don't want to see your fat face anywhere near my kitchen when I get home," it may be better to suggest, "I am planning to bake cookies this evening, and I wanted to make sure you weren't going to use the kitchen between six and eight o'clock."

Decide, also, how meals will be managed. If you do have little ones, you may be able to maintain a meals-together schedule. For us, we continued to eat like a family, even though we were in sort-of-single mode. We spent our evening meals focusing our attention on our daughter, which made sense, since we both worked and hadn't seen her during the day. It was hard to manage through that with a smile, but it was the right thing for our little one. It was all I could do to not lean across the table, steak knife poised in stabbing position, headed for his left temple. But with my sweet little three-year-old chomping innocently on carrot sticks just one seat away, I abstained. Instead, I repeated the mantra, "We are in the business of raising our daughter" over and over again. This reminded me that eating together was for her. It's important to note that if my former spouse weren't still living under the same roof as me, I would not have asked him to come over to eat meals. Our meal arrangement was simply a stopgap measure until he moved out. Otherwise, our daughter would have been wondering why Daddy stands over the kitchen sink to eat his frozen Tombstone pizza instead of sitting at the table with us.

MANTRAS to get you through the day

*We are in the business
of raising our child.*

A House Divided

Necessity may compel you to live under the same roof for longer than you'd like, which means that early on is the time to communicate, regardless of whether past communication consisted of him grunting at you while watching the Saturday Night Smack Down. Be clear about how things are different, even though you still share the same domain. Laundry, for example. I was dumbfounded that my ex continued to drop his dirty clothes in the hamper. My hamper, with my clothes, in my bathroom, that he no longer used every morning. Did he really think that I would do his laundry? His tightie-whities never were a turn on, but now the sight of them was simply repulsive. Would you toss your dirty clothes in your roommate's hamper? Didn't think so. Same rules apply. Keep your mom hat on, but replace your wife hat with a roommate hat, and let the rules of common courtesy between two near-strangers guide your thinking.

If one of you decides to move out soon after the divorce decision has been made, thereby avoiding the in-between-married-and-divorce limbo, I highly recommend going that route. This is hard, though, because it requires additional resources to allow for two living arrangements. But during this strange and highly charged time in your lives, living apart is sometimes the best route. This becomes an even easier choice when you don't have children, since fewer lives are impacted.

DIVORCED GIRLS' SOCIETY TENETS

✓ Load up the artillery with divorce experts: an attorney and a therapist.

✓ Surveillance and reconnaissance: Keep track of everything.

✓ Determine who is your ally and who's playing conscientious objector.

✓ Work out a temporary plan with the insurgent (ex living in your house)—a ceasefire while you work through the new boundaries.

Friends with Big (and Soggy) Shoulders

Like most women, I've always valued my girl-friends—particularly my college friends. Those were the keepers, in my mind. The ones I knew would always be there for me. During our eighteen years of friendship, I'd counted on my college gal pals, but I'd never sounded a critical call to action like this before. In college, there were those emotionally stressful moments where friends lent a shoulder or an ear. Things like the boyfriend breakups, the job offers not received, the STD from the one-night stand. But it was nothing that a little penicillin and late-night chats while enjoying a few tubes of chocolate-chip cookie dough couldn't solve. Crises were short term and easily remedied; friends were always close by.

The nice thing about a crisis in your younger years is that it always seemed to become fodder for a joke. Something that seemed quite devastating could actually make you laugh, thanks to a girlfriend. I had a friend who turned an embarrassing trip to the college clinic— to treat something you definitely would not want your mother to know you contracted—into a campus-wide April Fool's joke. Let me tell you, it went from pure panic to hysterical laughter in less time than it takes to say "communicable disease." From job-rejection letters delivered by prestigious *Fortune* 200 organizations, to bad LSAT scores, there was always a way to turn heartache into humor, which was how we were able to minimize the impact of the crisis.

Even when we were out of college, friends still played an important part of the day to day: Urgent phone calls were placed from the aisles of Ann Taylor (Jennifer determined the suede coat was a buy and actually bought one for herself, too); priority e-mails skipped across cyberspace as we decided between a rental house with a hot tub or beachside access; plans for the future revolved around our girls' weekends to New York, not when my husband would be moving out of the home we once shared. But our friendship had never been truly tested, was never required to see us through a truly life-altering situation like divorce.

Divorce is serious stuff. It's hard to know the boundaries—when fun can be poked and when it's best to sit back and listen without judgment. And that can be a tall order when your friend is dying to remind you of that night your ex got drunk and threw up in your favorite Coach briefcase. Your friends will definitely be put through the test during this particular life event.

What Your GIRLFRIEND *Is Thinking*

During our extended long-distance conversations, my end of the phone was silent except for some *uh-huh's*, a few *sure's*, and a couple of *absolutely's* thrown in for good measure. If being supportive meant I had to enforce my own gag order, then that's what I'd do. On those phone calls, I didn't add fuel to the fire, even though inside I was dying to shout, "Asshole! Kick his ass to the curb!" And every day that went by, every time I'd hang up the phone, I actually sensed that Vicki was in a better place than when she'd called, and I felt I'd done my job. I'd learned my first lesson as the friend of a divorcing woman: Shut up and listen.

The Dewey Decimal System of Friendship

You'll get a sense of what kinds of friends you'll want to keep close by in these early weeks. The ones who start calling and e-mailing more regularly than before, the ones who invite you to come stay at their house, those are the ones to lean on. Then there are the other ones. The ones who—I mean, this goes without saying, who wouldn't, right?—profess their love and adoration for you, feel terrible about the situation, but then can't wait to get off of the phone. ("Gosh, Vicki, I am so sorry to hear that your husband's left you, but my tomato plants haven't been watered all week, can I call you next Sunday?") Some girlfriends can't handle crises like this. They may be in fear for their own marriage, they may not know what to say, or what not to say, shortly after the news gets to them (they should buy this book—or lend it to them when you're done, okay?). Don't bother with them now. Put these people on hold, and concentrate on the one or two friends who have already donned their super-friend cape and are heeding the call of their girlfriend in need—these will become your Speed-Dial Sisters.

Taking Inventory without the Bar Codes

You've probably never had to conduct a mental inventory of all of your friends, but now is the time. It sounds so impersonal—how do you categorize a friend, catalog her pros and cons, her benefits and liabilities? But the real idea here is to figure out the strengths of your friendships and leverage those strengths when you need to. The friend who's always up for a cocktail, no matter what day of the week it is? Good to have. The friend who actually understands how to work the TiVo and has the patience to teach you? Invaluable. The friend who's always willing to lend an ear? That's one you should keep on speed dial.

You will be counting on girlfriends to keep you centered throughout this process, and to help give you the affirmation you formerly got from your spouse. I wanted—and needed—my friends to step in to pick up the spousal slack. Where I used to have plans to be with my husband on the weekends, I now needed invitations from friends to come visit. I needed the phone calls for no other reason than to have a friend say, "I haven't talked to you in a while, everything okay?" I needed the reminders that I was still the same person I'd always been, that I was still completely me, and nothing less than that.

Could there be girlfriends in your life who are not looking out for your best interest? Sure! Does the clichéd fair-weather friend really exist? Of course! Not everyone can take on the role of uber-friend, or is equipped to do so. And that's fine. It doesn't mean they're bad friends or that you need to cut ties and run; they just might not want to be the women you surround yourself with in the near future.

MANTRAS to get you through the day

I am that friend in need.

Girls You Do Not Want in Your Pledge Class

There will be girls who are not part of your pledge class. In fact, they will not even be given an invitation to bid. You can allow them to join the parties, just know that they won't be living in the beautiful brick sorority house. They won't know the secret handshake, and they will be relegated to the sterile dorm rooms across the quad. If you want, you can update them on a need-to-know basis. You might also consider putting them on your version of the Do Not Call list, and once this event has completed its course, perhaps you can pick up where you left off.

You may think your friends can't be labeled. And that's not what we're suggesting. Well, not *exactly*. But they can be put into categories that may help you decide who to call when you need an ear, and who to meet when you need a stiff drink.

The Angelina Jolie: This is the friend who makes you a bit uncomfortable because even though you think she's great fun, there's a tiny "Danger, Will Robinson" voice inside you every time you're with her. Her edginess is unnerving. She always left you wondering about her true agenda; confirmed when, upon announcing your news, she replies, "So you're saying your husband is single now?" The following long pause is accented by your sobs and her question, "Didn't you once tell me he thought I was hot?" Needless to say, this friend is not valuable right now. Keep her on the radar, though, she may be great fun to go out with once you are further along in embracing your single status.

The Poker: She's stoking the fire and getting you worked up. She'll at once reassure you about your decision, but then leave you second-guessing your ex with zingers like, "God, do you think he's screwing everything in sight?" Or she'll feign concern with an underhanded, "You deserve the best guy out there; I just hope you're not getting too old."

The Clueless: Upon the announcement, she tilts her head to the side and asks, "You were married?"

The Dismisser: She makes every crisis, no matter how dire, seem inconsequential, trite, and something that is easily overcome. This can sometimes be a healthy perspective, sort of an "in the grand scheme of things, does it really matter" point of view, which you may really need later on. But in the early part of your journey, you need someone a bit more sensitive to the situation at hand. She's the one who, when you call to talk about your divorce, interrupts your crying fits with a terse, "Hang on a sec, my other line's ringing."

The Obsesser: She can't get enough of your divorce. She asks for details, no matter how inappropriate. She can probe you about the dollar value of your husband's business without blinking an eye—and expect an answer, down to the penny. She also thinks that all you want to talk about is your divorce. It comes up every.single.time. you talk with her. When it's the last thing you want to talk about, she's making it front and center.

Your Pledge Class: Friends You Can Rely On
Now you know who won't be asked to join you for the ivy chain, but which friends *can* you rely on?

Identifying your pledge sisters is a big step forward. These are the women who will need to know where your hot buttons are and how to avoid pushing them, at least early on. If they know you secretly crave cigarettes during times like this, they won't "tsk, tsk" as you break out the pack of Marlboro Lights. But they might warn against making it a habit and hand you a piece of sugarless gum.

The Been There, Done That, Have the T-Shirt: This is the friend who has the script to divorce sitting on her bookshelf. She also starred in the play. She knows what you can expect, but what makes her a good friend is the way she is anticipating your upcoming emotional pitfalls, since she lived them as well. So, on your wedding anniversary, when you are reminded of your single status and are still not ready to accept it, she'll race over with a bottle of your favorite wine, lend an ear, and share some of her own hard-earned wisdom in the most positive way. She'll also break out some old pictures of the week you and she went on that trip to Cancun—to remind you that life was fun before your ex and there will be fun after him, too.

The Pep Squad: This is the friend who signs you up for hip-hop dance class, even though she knows you can barely chew gum and walk. She brings you to her oil-painting class and invites you to throw a pot at the local ceramics studio. Picasso you're not, but she wants you out there, having fun and enjoying life. She'll e-mail you the latest Web sites for Internet dating, and then she'll sit down and help write your dating profile. She may not have pompoms around her wrists, and she's long-outgrown saddle shoes, but her enthusiasm and zest for life is contagious, and she's great to have in your class because she reminds you that life is fun, and you are (gimme an) A-W-E-S-O-M-E.

The Pull-No-Punches: She's the one who will give you the real answers, and not coat them with pea-nut butter and coconut to make them taste sweeter. She will set you straight, because she keeps it real. So when you're on your second pint of Ben and Jerry's, she will tell you that your bikini from last summer was already pulling a bit at the sides, and added spoonfuls of Chunky Monkey isn't making it any better. In other words, she'll tell you what you need to hear, but don't want to. Her BS tolerance is low, so feeling sorry for yourself is not allowed. But more than that, she'll help you put things in their appropriate perspective. She's the friend you don't always want, but she is the one you sorely need.

Tips for Your SPEED-DIAL SISTERS

Sometimes honesty is not the best policy. Your friend is hurting enough right now; if she asks you a question and your *honest* answer will only cause her more pain, do you really need to speak the cold, hard truth? No, you can temper the truth with some encouraging words that will help her see the positive side of her life.

Q: "He said I was a bitch. Do you think I was a bitch?"
The truth: "Yeah. A raging bitch, in fact. I don't know how he put up with you this long."
A better answer: "There were times you both could have treated each other with more respect, but that's just part of being in a relationship."

Q: "Do you think he was cheating on me?"
The truth: "Hell yea, the guy was a walking herpes sore."
A better answer: "I don't know, and it really doesn't matter, because right now you need to be thinking about you, not him. Let's concentrate on getting through this."

Q: "Do you think I'll ever be happy again?"
The truth: "Not if you don't stop adopting cats and wearing those bunny slippers every day."
A better answer: "It probably won't happen tomorrow, but if you keep moving forward, it can only get better."

The Cool-Headed Sister: When you need someone to talk you down from the ledge, she's there with a megaphone. She knows exactly what to say. In her soothing voice, with her rational tone, she will help you realize that whatever you think is insurmountable isn't so bad after all. So when you call her and say, "My life is over, I have no friends, and my skin has more zits on it than the girl who babysits my daughter," she'll remind you that you are smart, loved, professionally successful, and a wonderful person. And those pimples? That's just from the Ben and Jerry's you devoured last night.

The No-Fly Zone

Officially, a no-fly zone is defined as "airspace in which certain aircraft, especially military aircraft, are forbidden to fly." Substitute friends for aircraft, husbands for military, and you see where this is going. The idea of a No-Fly Zone gives you the ability to set boundaries, albeit invisible to anyone but you, without looking like the bad guy. It gives you the opportunity to decide who would truly be helpful as you struggle through this situation, without feeling guilt and without fearing you'll come off like an ungrateful bitch.

Knowing where the No-Fly Zone begins and ends isn't easy. Its borders are constantly shifting, its edges blurry. The important thing here is for your friends and family to respect the fact that the Zone exists, to recognize that this safe area is necessary to keep your sanity intact, and that, ultimately, *you* determine the boundaries. Encourage your friends to ask when they're in doubt. This No-Fly Zone may lack the retaliatory threat of surface-to-air missiles, but when it comes to friendship, better safe than sorry.

Tips for Your SPEED-DIAL SISTERS

It can be awfully tempting to cast yourself in the role of savior, the friend charging in on your white horse to save the day. When Vicki told me about her situation, I wanted to help make it all better, I wanted to make her feel less alone and more included. But there was no getting around the fact that I was part of a couple and she was flying solo—and the last thing I wanted was to make her feel like the third wheel.

Good friends understand that a divorce isn't easy, and that's why it can become too easy to invite your divorcing girlfriend to come along to dinner, on vacation, or just come over to watch TV. Although an invitation is an assurance, or reassurance, that she's fun, if not more fun, than when she was a couple, invites should be handed out wisely. It's a good bet that an invitation to join a couple on an isolated Caribbean-beach getaway may make a divorcing girlfriend feel awkward. And chances are, once you're there with your husband and best friend, you'll discover that maybe this was one time you should have just sent a postcard.

So it's important for a Speed-Dial Sister to use a little common sense and forethought before tossing out invitations, and not feel obligated to include your divorcing friend just to show you care. And, likewise, you shouldn't feel slighted if your friend turns down a few offers. This isn't the *Love Boat*, after all, and you aren't Julie McCoy. It's not your job to play social director; it's just your job to let her know that there's a game of shuffleboard on the Lido deck—and let her take it from there.

I found many occasions in which to utilize, and, in my case, respect, the No-Fly Zone.

- My brother-in-law (my sister's husband) called and told me that he'd just received an invitation to join my estranged husband on his annual ski trip to Colorado. I invoked the No-Fly Zone, and my brother-in-law was able to decline knowing that he'd done the right thing by me.
- Jennifer's husband told her he wanted to call my future ex to tell him how sorry he was to hear the news. She immediately sat her husband down and explained the concept of the No-Fly Zone—that no matter how many times they'd rehashed the Red Sox World Series or bonded over the barbeque, he and my ex had no relationship beyond being the husbands of best friends, and calling now was flagrantly crossing the No-Fly Zone.

The Divorced Girls' Society
TOOLKIT

Your Reconnaissance Plan—Who's in and Who's Out

Better to institute the No-Fly Zone sooner rather than later. You'll avoid all sorts of uncomfortable questions and conversations, and possibly even hurt feelings.

Talk to your friends and family about the concept of a No-Fly Zone, and ask them to respect yours. Explain any topics/people you'd like to include in the No-Fly Zone, and ask that they steer clear until you're ready to remove the boundaries.

Topic/Person to Avoid

1. _____

2. _____

3. _____

4. _____

5. _____

What Your GIRLFRIEND *Is Thinking*

My friend was really getting divorced. And even though a part of me was still thinking that maybe they'd work things out, I wanted to stick by her. So how was I supposed to handle the sticky subject of her soon-to-be-ex? Did I tell her I never thought he was good enough for her (which was exactly what I was thinking)? That I hated the way he chewed his food and his taste in music sucked (so I didn't really know his taste in music that well, but it didn't really matter at that point)? Did I provide the ammunition she needed to think her new solo status was a good idea, even though I'd be risking that she'd hate me if they decided to work through their problems? How was I expected to help her when I didn't know if the next word out of my mouth would make her feel better or send her plummeting further into the depths of despair?

The No-Fly Zone: A Friend's Perspective

About a week after Vicki dropped the bomb, she came to me for some help. A guy friend of hers, "Bill," had sent an e-mail saying he'd heard about the situation and hoped they could still be friends. "Bill" hoped she knew that he still thought the world of her and he was there if she needed him. The message said all of the right things, hit all of the right notes, and included all of the positive buzz-phrases Vicki wanted to read, short of a smiley-faced emoticon at the end.

I know what you're thinking right now: *Aww, what a sweet guy.*

Wrong!

Sweet? Are you kidding me?

Did I mention that this "guy friend" was also her husband's *best friend*? That Vicki, her husband, and "Bill" actually purchased a beach house together, which, until her husband decided to bail out of his marriage, they'd shared on summer weekends? That "Bill" didn't just work for the same company as her husband, her husband was, in fact, "Bill's" *boss*?

Although he probably didn't know any better, what this guy did was wrong. Why? Because it made him feel better, not her. Because all it did was put her in the position of either coming across like a bitch if she didn't respond, or looking completely pathetic for clinging to the friendship of a man who, at that very moment, was probably hoisting a gin and tonic with her estranged husband. Because even though "Bill" thought he was extending an olive branch, for Vicki it was more like a tangled vine of poison ivy. It was divorce's version of friendly fire.

So while I listened to Vicki debate whether or not she should reply to his e-mail, I decided that it was time to come up with some rules of engagement, some guidelines that I could follow to ensure that I didn't make similar mistakes in the name of friendship. After all, although the situation hadn't reached the fever pitch of *The War of the Roses,* where Michael Douglas and Kathleen Turner hang from the crystal chandelier in their entryway during an especially bitter divorce (Vicki had assured me that, after discovering her homebuilder's cost-saving shortcuts, she wasn't willing to test the fortitude of their foyer lighting fixture), she was about to enter into battle. She needed allies she could trust, people she could count on to be in her corner. True friends who'd dig in for the long haul and provide unconditional, unwavering support, not people who simply say all of the right things, but aren't there to help her through the midnight crying jags.

And if there was one thing I was sure of, it was that the best friend of a soon-to-be-ex-husband can't pretend he's Switzerland when the ex-husband signing the separation agreement is also signing his paycheck.

So, instead of shutting up, I told her what I thought. And you know what? She discovered she agreed. And I discovered that there are times you really should give your honest opinion. It doesn't mean she has to agree with you or follow your advice, but it lets her know that you're not simply her yes-man; you can be relied on to give honest answers, too.

The Friend with Benefits
Yes, it's what you think it is. And guess what? It's okay to have one—if you can handle it. Make sure you can before you go down that road. Because as great as it sounds, laying your head on another man's naked chest after having sex might feel a tad odd, considering the situation. And even if you can deal with the fact that you're actually having sex with someone other than your

husband, your friend might not be able to. After all, here he is enjoying the pleasures of the flesh with you, and the last thing he wants to talk about is whether or not he thinks your husband might be bipolar, or if the way you insisted on being on top all of the time drove him away. In fact, this friend might not want to hear anything at all about what's going on between you and the man he's replaced in bed.

If you're lucky enough to not only find a friend with benefits, but to also choose one who wants to hear about what's going on with your divorce, then by all means, talk. Talk until the cows come home. But perhaps this particular "friend" is not someone you want to be sharing your divorce details with. If you're closing your eyes in what he thinks is ecstasy and what you know is avoidance, it's time to think about *why* you're there in the first place.

It's possible that the affection of the opposite sex will remind you how sexy and interesting you are. *A good thing.* Or, it's possible it may remind you that your boobs have descended two inches in the past ten years, and instead of using that mirror to enjoy Hugh Hefner–worthy escapades, you're checking out the reflection of the out-of-shape woman with the tears in her eyes. *Not such a good thing.* Are you really ready to have sex with a man who means nothing to you? Or worse, are you ready to have sex with a man to whom you mean nothing? If you can separate sex from everything going on in your life, then you should absolutely consider this option, and allow yourself to have fun with no strings attached. But if you're attempting to use sex to fix what's going on, I'd suggest you find a different extracurricular activity you can enjoy with your clothes on.

I had thought about recruiting an "FWB"—I hadn't had sex in what was going on about a year, and my primal urges were getting the best of me. I had also heard that great sex starts after thirty-five for most women. I had separated at thirty-six—this great-sex concept had eluded me thus far. So the need was certainly there.

The challenge for me, though, was that I had a whole host of emotional issues to contend with too, and I was unable to isolate just the physical part to allow myself that FWB. I wasn't sure if I would turn into a psychotic looney-toon if my FWB didn't call the next day, didn't hold me for thirty minutes after the deed was done, and didn't send me a stuffed teddy on Valentine's Day. In other words, I was unable to determine what, exactly, I'd want out of an FWB. And as much as I wanted to have sex, I was more afraid I'd get caught up in more than sex, and that would be too complicated for me right now.

Did I want hot monkey sex? Sure. But not badly enough to take on all of the other emotional pitfalls that might have ensued. With the right "friend" and expectations, this could actually be a good outlet, but I didn't have that kind of friend, and I wasn't willing to take on any added stress.

Embarking on a friend with benefits situation before you're ready could set off a host of complications in your life, and as I've reiterated throughout, your life is complicated enough—no need to pile on. Some examples of not being ready include: crying jags while undressing in front of your FWB; choosing to wear the black Victoria's Secret negligee you bought for your honeymoon, and then describing the details of said honeymoon to your friend; providing directions that use your ex as a compass, for example, "My ex used to like it when I did that with my finger, do you like that, too?"; or using the post-coital afterglow to rehash your marriage and all of its disappointments. That's why you have a therapist, and she doesn't require that you get naked to do the rehashing.

The Divorced Girls' Society
GOLDEN RULES

While a friend with benefits sounds great—conversation and mind-blowing sex—it's not as uncomplicated as it sounds. In fact, you better be damn sure you know what you're doing if you choose to go this route.

- Do think over the consequences—both mental and physical.
- Do get a second opinion from a friend (not the FWB, another friend)—someone who can give you an honest reaction.
- Do make sure you are able to compartmentalize sex—and that your FWB can do the same.
- Don't go into this expecting that you've found your one true love. Ever hear of the rebound?
- Don't use your friend as a sort of revenge tactic—it doesn't work in the movies, and in real life it's just tacky. Besides, it's not fair to you or him.

While an FWB may seem like a relatively simple fix to a pretty common problem, there may be even easier ways to solve the "I need sex" conundrum. Toys, for example, can be great substitutes for the FWB. These are fundamental needs we're talking about here, and getting those needs filled (no pun intended) can be accomplished with a variety of sex accoutrements. And if an FWB actually seems like too much of a commitment, the one-night stand, however cliché, might also get you back to your happy place. As long as you recognize what the potential consequences are, both the up side and down side. Since we're all adults here, you'll have to use your best judgment in deciding how and when it's appropriate for you to satisfy your carnal cravings. As with all choices in life, there are tradeoffs. Now, go forth and conquer those sexual needs in the way that suits you best. No need to repress them; the last thing you need in addition to the emotional turmoil of the end of your marriage is a hearty dose of sexual frustration.

DIVORCED GIRLS' SOCIETY TENETS

✓ Take inventory of your friends and determine the best way to leverage their strengths; build your Society.

✓ Recognize that not every friend can offer you the same level of support—but that doesn't mean they're not still your friends.

✓ Determine your No-Fly Zone and let friends and family know that it exists.

✓ Your Pledge Class sisters are in your special internal circle now—they should be called upon as often as needed—yes, even at 3 A.M. After all, that's why they've made the cut.

Going Public:
Announcing Your New Status to the Rest of the World

Telling friends and family is one thing; they love you. They can offer a reassuring hug, a shoulder to lean on, and they may even offer you a home-cooked meal. But telling the world at large? That's an entirely different story.

Why was the idea of telling neighbors, cowork-ers, and other acquaintances so daunting for me? Quite simply, I didn't want to be judged. I didn't want to be pitied or placed into the category of *divorced woman*. I didn't want them to look at me differently. I didn't want to become known as "Vicki, the one going through the divorce." I wanted to continue being known as "Vicki, the hot babe with the rockin' bod." Okay, seriously. I just wasn't ready to take my news public. The public, after all, didn't know me as well as my friends and family. Worse, I had no way of knowing how they'd react. It's a big unknown, and unknowns are scary. The element of not being able to control or anticipate reactions can be enough to want to avoid this part of your divorce altogether. Me, I started slow.

But before I broke the news, I started with my daughter. As with all things child related, safety checks should be in place. As ironic as this might sound, make sure your child knows the news before the neighbors. The last thing you need is for the six-year-old bully across the street to be the first to tell your son about his mommy and daddy breaking up, because you know he won't do it in a neutral, unbiased way. He's six. And did I mention he's a bully? Tell the children, then tell the neighbors. With both, keep it simple. You want your children insulated from neighborhood gossip; so report the news, and leave out the editorializing.

Howdy, Neighbor

Generally speaking, neighbors are an innocuous bunch. They're probably people similar to you. I mean, you all decided to live in the same place, right? Your children all play together, and you've seen them at the summertime block parties, progressive dinners, and the occasional, dreaded candle party. Because they get a front-row seat to all of the goings-on at your house, they may have already noticed that things are different. Maybe one car isn't in the driveway as often as it used to be. Maybe they've observed that one of you isn't around as much anymore. Or maybe the sudden presence of Larry's Lawn Service is the big clue, because the person who's MIA has been slacking on the lawn duty. The thing is, no matter how normal you think things appear on the outside, they're your neighbors, and that means they pay attention to what's going on next door. Their property value depends on it. So it shouldn't come as a big shocker when you break the news, and you may just be confirming the buzz. So starting close to home is a good, relatively safe place to begin.

Step One: Keep It Simple, Sister

When breaking the news, keep the story as neutral as possible. Rather than, "Yeah, the poor guy, who knew someone with such an overtly masculine personality was repressing his cross-dressing tendencies? Turns out he owns more black pumps than I do. I do hope he gets help." Try something like, "We're no longer together, but he's doing well and so am I." Your neighbors don't need details, and if you and your ex are both still living in the same house, it would be unfair to influence your neighbors to start siding with one of you; it'll just make things even more awkward. If they probe, you are totally within your rights to end the conversation with an, "I'd rather not discuss the details." Unfortunately, step two may require you to say that more often than you had hoped.

Step Two: Don't Fan the Flames

They don't call them nosy neighbors for nothing. Know that once the news is out, the questions will start. People will want to know more. So don't fuel the cul-de-sac fire—try to respond to questions with the same unbiased, objective tone with which you broke the news. They probably have their own theories anyway, regardless of how you position it. The lady across the street will remember when your husband ignored her wave that one morning—the rude bastard. The guy next door will remember that night he saw a strange car in your driveway while your husband was away on business. Do you need to explain that the blue Ford Taurus belonged to the exterminator who was providing a quote to extinguish the fleas your dog brought into bed with you? I don't think so.

So when you're out planting tulip bulbs one afternoon and you see the woman from the white house with red shutters whispering to the woman from the brick colonial, just smile and give them a friendly wave. They may be trying to deconstruct what's really going on in your house, or they might just be commenting on last summer's daffodil debacle, but it doesn't matter. Leave them guessing. Leave them wondering if you've got a twenty-two-year-old lover planting his own daffodils in a more secluded space.

Step Three: Don't Dish It Out in Installments

Your life is not a soap opera, but after the announcement your neighbors will inevitably be waiting for the second installment of (cue dramatic organ music) *The Divorce Next Door*. Don't do it. Unless your next-door neighbor happens to be your best friend, in which case she'll know better, there is no need to answer those "How's it going?"s with "Well, let me tell you what's going on with the distribution of our assets." It just isn't necessary. As tempting as it may be to take this polite inquiry of your well-being as an invitation to unload, resist the urge. A simple, "Things are well, thank you" will do just fine. And eliminate any speculation that the stares you're getting at the mailbox are due to the fact that the entire street knows that your soon-to-be-ex-husband waxed his back.

And, remember, you'll really only need to tell one neighbor. Big news like the end of a marriage is the neighborhood equivalent of gonorrhea—and it will spread just as rapidly.

The Divorced Girls' Society
GOLDEN RULES

- Do keep the breakup news neutral—resist the temptation to point fingers, especially the middle one.
- Do assume that word will travel, whether you want it to or not.
- Do prepare for questions and inappropriate responses, but don't respond with a weekly newsletter promising real-time coverage of unfolding events.
- Don't go into too much detail—do people really need to know that he left a half tube of Preparation H behind in the medicine cabinet when he moved out?
- Don't feel the need to tell everyone—the Fed Ex driver and that guy who sells newspapers on the corner don't really need to know that your husband's side of the bed is empty.
- Don't take it personally, rehearse your answers in advance, and remember that there's nothing wrong with saying you'd rather not discuss it.

Change Management in the Workplace, Otherwise Known as, "I'm Getting Divorced!"

The workplace has its own unique set of considerations. While there are very clear policies and procedures to help employees through many major life events, there's not much that helps when you're going through a divorce; though, as you can probably attest at this point, it's about as big a life change as you can imagine. Possibly, your company offers an employee-assistance program, which may be an alternative to therapy, but after that, you're on your own. But consider this: You get a bereavement day when your grandma dies, you get maternity leave when there's a bun in the oven, you get floating holidays to celebrate whatever religion you choose, and you get sick days when you're puking your guts out. But where's the help when the reason you're feeling sick to your stomach is that your husband just laid claim to your favorite antique credenza?

For the most part, the protocol around divorce hasn't been established yet. There aren't any signs outlining helpful tips hanging in the company cafeteria next to instructions on how to perform the Heimlich maneuver and reminders to sort your recyclables. So the questions float out there: Do I tell my boss? Do I ask for time off? It's not that corporate America is in denial about this event; it's more that there's no established system in place—so you need to use your judgment here. It makes sense to tell the boss about a bun in the oven because you'll need time off, and maybe there is the option of flex time in your future. And of course you share information about an upcoming wedding and subsequent honeymoon. Same goes for acceptance into the executive MBA program. Divorce doesn't exactly elicit the same high-fives and department cupcakes, but the ramifications of your situation can have a much greater impact on your office conduct.

Talk about distractions. If you thought you had trouble concentrating when you knew there was only one Twix bar left in the candy machine, imagine how difficult it will be to keep your mind on work now that there are a million other divorce-related things to occupy your mind. Zoning out in meetings? You're no longer imagining sunning your buns on a tropical beach, but imagining that you'll never be able to afford another vacation after this is over. Staring vacantly at rows of numbers on a spreadsheet until they all blend together? You're not picturing last night's sexcapade, but last night's teary breakdown while you flipped through old photo albums. Sometimes work can help take your mind off what's going on outside the four walls of your office, and if so, maybe you want to keep the line drawn. But if you're having trouble separating what's happening in your personal life from how it's affecting your professional life, maybe it's time to tell someone so they don't just think you've lost the ability to sit through a meeting without wailing into your coffee cup.

Coming Clean without Giving up the Dirt

A divorce takes time. There are meetings with attorneys, therapist appointments, court commitments. And then, of course, there are the occasions that you don't schedule, but that creep up on you anyway. Like those awkward moments when a coworker discovers you sobbing over the copy machine and thinks you're taking this low toner thing way too personally.

MANTRAS to get you through the day

I'm not running for public office.

I grappled with what to disclose. Knowing I might be out of the office more than usual, knowing that I might be a bit emotionally frail, I wondered if I should set expectations that I would be out of sorts for a while. Maybe it was appropriate to ask for some slack around the office. Should I hold a meeting in the conference room and tell all? Or did I want to keep everything to myself? Communicating the end of a marriage is one of those things that people have various opinions on. I, for one, happened to be most judgmental about those divorcing—obviously somebody had to do something wrong; people just didn't get divorced out of the blue. There had to be a skeleton in the closet, right?

My own reaction to other couple's divorces made me that much more sensitive to what people would think of my situation. Okay, let's be honest here. What I really worried about was what they would think of *me*. Was I difficult to live with? Did I have a wandering eye? Was I leaving my husband for a younger version of Antonio Banderas, or was my husband leaving me for an older version of Paris Hilton?

Obviously, my fear of people's responses played a big role in how I decided to handle things at work. And how I decided to handle things was to downplay what was going on. And by *downplay* I mean I didn't tell anyone. Not even the HR person when my husband and I needed a notary public to witness our signatures when we refinanced our (now *my*) home. I went to the office every single day and acted as if everything was status quo at home. When coworkers asked what I did over the weekend, I'd answer honestly. "I took my daughter to Washington, D.C., and we went to the zoo." If they just happened to assume that "we" included the father of my child, well, that was their assumption. I didn't make up stories about the fabulous family moment around the Christmas tree, and instead told people the truth—my holidays were festive and Santa found his way down our chimney just fine.

Whether they noticed how vague my answers had become I couldn't tell you, because nobody ever mentioned that the photo of my husband miraculously disappeared from my desk and was replaced with my daughter's school picture.

Luckily, it wasn't out of character for me—I am generally a private person at work. So it made sense that this would be kept a private matter—at least early on—until I was comfortable going full disclosure. When was that, you ask? Is there a point of no return where you have to 'fess up? Was it at a weekly meeting, and the icebreaker was, "When did you meet your significant other and how long have you been together?" Was it to be revealed when a coworker asked if my last name was mine or my husband's? That point of no return never happened for me; I was always able to deflect those kinds of questions and do the big reveal when I was ready. I was able to choose when, how, and to whom I told the news. But if I'd been nominated for Employee of the Year and the lovely woman in HR wanted to know where to send my husband's invitation to the watch-giving ceremony, I would have politely informed her that my husband and I were no longer together. Really, I would have. There was no award or ceremony to force my hand, however, so I kept it to myself for a long time. A really, really long time.

I was manic about managing my marital situation in the workplace. It was the DefCon six of damage control. A full court press. I refused to let anyone at work know what I was going through. Which was dumb, in retrospect, and you have the benefit of my stupidity. I was determined to follow a policy of Don't Ask, Don't Tell. Except I went one step further and actually continued to wear my wedding band months after my husband and I had been living apart. Coworkers asked about my weekend plans, what my husband and I were doing for the holidays, and my answers never gave away the reality that my plans included dropping my daughter off at my husband's apartment and heating up a Lean Cuisine while watching reruns of *Beverly Hills 90210*.

What Your GIRLFRIEND Is Thinking

She's still wearing her wedding band to work? None of her coworkers have a clue that she's spending her Saturday nights with Kelly, Dylan, and Brandon Walsh at the Peach Pit? Come on, just tell the people, already! What's the big deal?

I know what you're thinking—this chick has issues and *she's* telling *me* what to do? But I didn't see what I was doing as dishonest. I wasn't lying; I just wasn't exactly telling the whole story. It was the mother of all façades, and it kept me on my toes. But it also allowed me to spend forty hours a week in a divorce-free zone, where no one asked me how the separation was going or whether my daughter was adjusting or if I'd signed up for the latest Internet dating site yet. I could exist without the distraction of this thing called divorce. To my coworkers, I was still the same person I had always been, and the fact that my marriage was over was immaterial, because, frankly, it was deliberately left out. At work I was the same old Vicki I'd always been, and there was something reassuring about that as I drove to the office every day. My job had become the one place where things didn't seem to change.

Except it didn't occur to me until too late that living these dual lives requires planning, thinking, and a significant amount of preparation. So when the Christmas party invitations arrived and I realized that I couldn't go it alone lest I be publicly outed, I made up an excuse that involved a nonexistent ninetieth birthday party for my very existent grandmother. How could I attend a corporate holiday boozefest when Grammy was celebrating her ninth decade? I had an airtight excuse. And it worked fine. Except the following year Grammy really did have a ninetieth birthday party—on the same night as the company holiday party. And so continues the web of deceit, and the confused look on your boss's face when he could have sworn your grandmother turned ninety last year. It was all stupid and unnecessary, but for some reason I felt compelled to keep this part of my life top secret. What's that saying? "What a tangled web we weave when first we practice to deceive," or, as my five-year-old would say more succinctly, "Liar, liar, pants on fire."

In hindsight, I probably should have told people at work sooner rather than later. It just would have been easier in the long run. But at the time, I did what felt right—and when it comes to managing through divorce, allowing yourself to trust your gut can go a long way to feeling in control of the situation. So whether you decide to simply quietly move the vacation photos of last year's trip to Myrtle Beach off your desk, or you notify everyone via interoffice memo that you'll be changing back to your maiden name, what you do is your call. What matters the most is that you're able to continue working without distraction. You may want to put it out there sooner than I chose to. Rip off the Band-Aid, get it over with, and get on with your life. If you have a close friend at work, tell her, and then ask her to leak it out as necessary. The word may get out that way, without you having to make the effort to communicate it. If, however, getting the news out means you'll be wondering if the receptionist is smiling at you or heckling your obvious inability to be loved by another human being, perhaps it's best to wait.

I eventually removed the gold and diamond bands from around my left ring finger and waited patiently to react to the inevitable question about where the rings went. I knew that it would only require telling one or two people before my marital dissolution would become common knowledge. (News like that is juicy stuff—it's what water-cooler conversations are made of.) One art director in my department finally posed the question, and my long-rehearsed response, "I'm not wearing them anymore because I'm getting divorced," rolled off my lips in a most emancipating way. And just as I suspected, in a few short days it seemed that most knew. Which probably explains why the bald fat guy in IT ogled at me for the next several weeks as I worked my way through the salad bar in the cafeteria.

What about the Rest of the World?

You probably never thought you'd need Mapquest to plan out your divorce communication strategy, but the proximity of your acquaintances plays a large role in determining when and how you break the news. Here's the thing: You probably have a 20–25-mile radius of people who you interact with pretty regularly. Assuming they are people you care about, and that you actually want to tell them, start with the small circle and consider notifying those parties first. And as with the neighbors (those closest in your geo-mapping survey), keep the news as simple as possible. Realize, also, that sometimes your news will be proactive, sometimes reactive—for instance, when the guy behind the counter at the Wok In casually comments on how he thought your husband hated chicken fried rice (he does, make it a double).

Reactive vs. Proactive

You'll need to determine the communication tactic you leverage—whether you go offensive or defensive. Your choice will depend on frequency of interaction, the importance that information has on said recipient of information, and how much a part of your life that person is to you.

There is the Italian restaurant on Main Street where Angelo and Josephina, his adoring wife, would serve you every Wednesday night, not even bothering to ask what you wanted; instead, bringing out the sausage and olive pizza and carafe of Chianti as if on auto pilot. They saw you pregnant, they cooed when you brought your three-week-old daughter in, they met your in-laws and sister. They recommended the piano teacher you now rely on to get your child to Carnegie Hall. They know you, and they are pretty familiar with your family. So they'll probably notice that your ex is conspicuously absent from the Wednesday night visits. You don't need to call attention to it, but if brought up while serving a slice, you'll need to respond accordingly. This would fall into the reactive bucket. A curious, "Where's your husband tonight?" is easily nipped in the bud with a casual, "Probably working, but I couldn't be positive; we're separated." Enough said.

Your child's teacher, however, definitely requires proactive communication. Make sure your child's teacher knows about the family situation. In this case, more than any, neutrality is best. Your child's teacher does not want to hear, "My current husband couldn't satisfy my needs so I've left him for Lorenzo—aka the Tango Tickler—and I want to make sure you knew that my son is still adjusting to this." Better to simply state that things at home are in flux, and one parent is no longer living there.

Another proactive approach you can take with people you want to inform, but who you don't want to pick up the phone to tell, would be to communicate the situation through your annual Christmas card or holiday communication. If your holiday picture doesn't have your ex in there, then most people will put one and one together (or, in this case, subtract one from one). In my annual holiday letter I didn't make a direct reference to my newly single status, but my stories about what happened throughout the year only included myself and my daughter, implying, pretty clearly, that things had changed.

There's Always Someone Left to Tell

You've told your neighbors, your family, and your close friends. All that's left are those on the fringes of your life. People like former coworkers with whom you still keep in occasional contact. You meet for lunch a few times a year, and send e-mails about job opportunities that you think she may be interested in. For this type of friend, revealing the big life change can happen at your next lunch meeting, because there's no real rush to get the news out any sooner. So the next time you're meeting Alison from R&D at Olive Garden, as you dine on your unlimited soup and salad, tell her the news, but keep it light. Just like the friendship.

Your dentist. I bring this up because if you think about it, most married couples share a dentist. For three straight visits over the course of a year and a half the receptionist asked, after I scheduled my daughter's appointment, if I wanted to make my ex's next appointment as well. I shrugged it off with a nonchalant, "Better to let him take care of it; I don't know his schedule," when what I really wanted to say was, "I hope his teeth fall out." Finally, after the third appointment that took place during our separation, I casually responded to the receptionist's request with an, "Actually, we're not married anymore. If you'd like, I can give you his new phone number so you can contact him directly about his appointments." With that one simple line, I'd ensured that the receptionist would never ask me about his plaque-crusted molars again.

What you may start to notice is that many times there are these perfect little opportunities to reveal the change, so take advantage of those. Remember that even though it gets easier each time you tell one more person, it is your call to decide who you tell and when.

DIVORCED GIRLS' SOCIETY TENETS

✓ Map out your communication plan, keeping it within the 20–25-mile radius.

✓ Proactive or reactive? Depends on the person and what that person will do with that information.

✓ Revealing your divorcing status at work should be planned out, done thoughtfully, and in a way that works best for you.

✓ You can't control your public. But you're not Sally Field, so you don't care if they really, really like you or not. Let them know, but don't stress about their reaction.

The Five Stages, or If It's Tuesday, This Must Be Denial

Just when I thought there were no more tears left to cry, the waterworks started again and proved me wrong. Something as innocuous as a CNN report from Rome triggered teary flashbacks of the warm May evening my husband and I strolled through St. Peter's Square sharing a chocolate gelato cone. Yes, even the creamiest chocolate ice cream could no longer give me pleasure. Damn him. My emotional mood swings made PMS look downright enjoyable. But old clichés exist for a reason, and as time passed the wounds may not have been healed, but they were a little less raw. The emotional swings were smaller and less often. Still doesn't explain why I momentarily imagined my partner coming home from work on April first with a big stuffed dog in one arm and a bouquet in the other, hollering from the door,

"Honey, Happy April Fool's . . . I really had ya, didn't I? Pretty clever joke, huh? Pretend to not want to be married anymore; I'm one wild and crazy guy!" Not. My therapist reassured me that it was completely normal to feel what I was feeling—or not feeling. And believe it or not, knowing that I was normal—a basket case, but normal—was a big relief.

MANTRAS to get you through the day

I'm not going crazy.

When you're pregnant, you run out to buy that irksome (but comfortingly predictable) book on what you should expect when you're expecting. Wouldn't it be great if the same kind of owner's manual existed for those of us going through the emotional ups and downs of divorce, a book that explained how you'd feel sadness between weeks eighteen and twenty, and then, like a baby springing from your loins, all sadness would be expelled from your body. It would go on to chart your emotional progress, citing defined starts and hard stops around the different stages of grief. You'd know when it would begin, when it would be done, and you could cross each state off your list once and for all. And there. It's done. Wipe your hands clean and call it a day. There'd be an end state, a finality. You may have already checked the bookstores for this book, and are as frustrated as the rest of us that it just doesn't exist.

While signed divorce papers are a pretty good indication that your marriage has come to its end, your emotional state doesn't follow a timetable. It may be over in the eyes of the law, but your heart may still be in month fourteen of a thirty-six-month recovery. Or maybe you've outpaced the legal system and you are in full recovery and acceptance, even though the great state of New Jersey and Judge Bigbelly have yet to slam down the gavel and declare you free and clear. Each woman has her own way of experiencing the stages, her own pace at which she'll go through the emotions. Some of us race through the feelings, while others do it with tortoise-like speed. But divorce isn't a race, we don't get team shirts and a medal for crossing the finish line (although if we did, mine would be sleeveless and pink and declare "I'm #1" on the back).

He's Dead to Me, So Why Is He Living Down the Street in Apartment 2B?

Research suggests that divorce creates the emotional, psychological, and physical stress second only to the death of a loved one. Similarly, you go through the same five emotional stages: denial, anger, bargaining, depression, and acceptance (of course, it took Elisabeth Kübler-Ross—a woman—to figure that one out). Although most women want a road map to tell them what to expect and when, when it comes to divorce and the accompanying emotions, there's no timeline, only time. And even though Kübler-Ross may have figured out *what* we can expect, *when* we can expect it is a different story. And while the when can't be neatly defined, the good news is that the whens get more and more infrequent as time goes on.

For me, I wanted each and every stage to have a beginning, a middle, and an end. With laser-like precision, I

Tips for Your SPEED-DIAL SISTERS

One thing I didn't want to do was begin acting differently. I didn't want Vicki to think that I was treating her any differently than I did before she announced the split. The key word here is sensitivity. A friend describing in intimate detail the romantic weekend at a bed and breakfast—the way she gazed into her husband's eyes, proclaimed her love, and then went crazy in the bedroom—probably isn't such a great idea. However, even though Vicki was going through a divorce, I learned that there is some comfort to knowing the rest of the world hasn't changed as much as her own. She didn't begrudge her friend's happiness; in fact, she found it reassuring. So keep telling the stories—romantic ones, silly ones, whatever. With so much uncertainty going on in your girlfriend's life, sharing stories of happy times, stability, and regularity are welcome reminders that even though her own life is changing, life goes on.

wanted to be able to identify what I was going through and where it fell in the linear progression. Problem was, it wasn't linear. Sometimes it was a continuum, and there I was, circling laps on the anger merry-go-round. I'm sure there are cases where women skip right over depression and go right into bargaining mode—*If I forgo this slice of cheesecake, the judge will award me the sports car.* The only certainty is the randomness with which emotions will occur. So don't drive yourself crazy trying to figure it all out, trying to plan your emotional response. Just know that the emotions will come, you'll get through them, and you'll come out better at the other end.

What Your GIRLFRIEND Is Thinking

Just when Vicki's marriage was coming to an end, I was celebrating eleven years of marital bliss (okay, bliss may be overdoing it, but you know what I mean). Things in my life were going well, no major complaints. But when we talked or e-mailed, I was afraid to tell her this. When she asked about the vacation my husband and I took to a tropical island, how could I tell her it was amazing, wonderful, and not think about the fact that her Caribbean vacations with her husband had come to an end? If I held my husband's hand or kissed him in front of her, would she hate me for it? Could I be happy in front of her without feeling like my good fortune only highlighted the turmoil on her doorstep?

On the one hand I wanted to show that I empathized with the situation, but on the other, because I hadn't been through it myself, I really didn't know what she was going through. I had no idea how to act. Was I rubbing it in by talking about my own divorce-free life?

It's Just a Stage

The bad news is that there are five stages. The good news is that adolescence isn't one of them. If all goes well, you'll come out of this without a single acne scar, and the knowledge that you made it out alive without once sniffing your underarms to see if you smell. The five stages include some pretty heady emotional states, but they all serve a purpose as you manage your emotional recovery.

Stage 1: Denial

This is your inner psyche's way of protecting you from being overwhelmed by the bad stuff you're going through. It's your temporary shield from reality. It's like nature's little way of saying, "You're too frail to see that this is a whopper of a big deal happening, so for now, you can pretend it's not." You can't take it all in at once, that would be freak-out city. So your brain plays a little game with you, called denial. And while people make fun of this emotional state, it exists for a reason, and going through it is completely normal and healthy.

Believe it or not, sometimes it's okay to be in denial, like when it helps you get through the early stages of "the big life change." But when denial prevents you from progressing to the next stage of grief, you've been in denial too long, and, Houston, we've got a problem.

- **Unhealthy denial:** You Photoshop a picture of your husband into your Christmas photograph with the tagline, "Our thirteenth Christmas together! Merry Christmas from us to you!" and it goes to all sixty-three people on your mailing list. Not only is that unhealthy, it's a little weird. Get that therapist of yours on speed dial.
- **Healthy denial:** One month after your breakup, you get an invitation to your second cousin's wedding. You can't bear the thought of attending it alone, so you RSVP no with a vague excuse that includes polyester allergies and irritable-bowel syndrome.

Denial can be a useful coping mechanism, as long as it doesn't stifle your progress—which means you shouldn't allow yourself to linger in Stage 1 for too long.

Stage 2: Anger

Ooooh, anger, that dirty little word. Nothing but negative connotations, bitter women sucking down tequila shots while muttering phrases like "pencil dick" and "couldn't find a G-spot if he had a Sherpa." Anger must be bad, right? Wrong. Anger is a fundamental part of the healing process when going through loss. Is it a license to pitch large ceramic plates across the room and watch them shatter against the wall? Scream like a hyena in heat and slam your fist through a glass window? Actually, yes, that's exactly what it means. There are some who don't need to act out to express anger, and others who need to be overt about it. Since anger follows denial in the process, generally it's a release of the emotions that were bottled up while you were in denial, and now you're letting them out—big time. So as long as small children and pregnant women are not within arm's reach, have at it with your rage. Get it all out of your system. Remember, it's therapeutic. And baby, you're entitled.

- **Unhealthy Anger:** You go to that creepy Wiccan store in town and stock up on eye of newt and an out-of-print copy of *Death Spells and Rituals*. At home, you've turned your lobster pot into a cauldron, and your wardrobe is beginning to look more and more like Stevie Nicks's. Nothing against Wiccans, but if you are taking on new religions and practicing death spells, I'm thinking bad, right? Anger should be releases of energy and emotions, not plotting and planning and casting spells.
- **Healthy Anger:** Know that Waterford vase that your mother-in-law gave you and your ex to celebrate your first year of wedded bliss? You never

really liked it anyway. Go ahead, toss it in the metal garbage can. Won't that sound brilliant? Imagine your next kickboxing class, where the punching bag morphs into your ex's face. Have at it; you'll be expressing your anger, and your ass will also benefit. Online message boards are also great places to unleash a tirade of what's bothering you. They're as anonymous as you want them to be, you are purging the thoughts from your system, and you have an audience waiting to hear it. You can have a lot of fun expressing some healthy anger. It can be as physical or passive as you want it to be.

Stage 3: Bargaining

For the shopper in all of us, what could be better than a bargain? Bargaining is typically a positive word. You bargain for a better deal, you strike a bargain and walk away with a purse for 25 percent less than the tag dangling from its strap—you shrewd girl, you! But in the context of grief, unfortunately, it's a desperate attempt to try and reverse whatever bad event is imminent. And, no, bargaining doesn't mean you hold a garage sale and offer up his favorite keepsakes at rock-bottom prices. It's your psyche's way of saying, "I am willing to make trade-offs and negotiate—no matter how bad a tradeoff it may be—in order to not let this thing see itself through."

For your divorce, bargaining may take on the form of negotiating with your ex on problems and issues that previously were the ones that drove you over the edge. What may have been the most offensive and disgusting habit before, all of a sudden becomes a minor, hardly noticeable irritation. If you've initiated the divorce, then you may be using bargaining to mentally talk yourself out of what it was that made you want to leave him in the first place. *That extreme fighting habit that's drained your bank account left him with eight-and-a-half fingers and resulted in a detached retina? Maybe it's simply his way of letting off a little steam after a long day at the office.* And if your ex is the one who wants out, you might use bargaining to get him to reconsider his decision. Bargaining can be viewed as a sort of last-ditch attempt before coming to terms with the fact that what's happening, is truly happening.

Remember, though, that bargaining won't actually change anything. It's simply a tricky coping mechanism that distorts your thinking process. Face it, the only real valuable bargaining is the kind you get at DSW during their buy-one-get-one-half-off sale. So if you find yourself thinking, *Quick, what else can I do to make this boogeyman go away?* remember that it's all part of the emotional journey toward that big finale: acceptance. And don't, under any circumstances, let him turn your living room into the ultimate fighting arena.

- **Bad Bargaining:** He's uncommunicative, always has been. It was like talking to a baloney sandwich, only not nearly as satisfying. But maybe, just maybe, that means he's the strong, silent type? Maybe he's expressive in other ways; you just haven't picked up on those other ways yet. Maybe the way he deftly swings his golf clubs is his way of communicating. Or the way he shampoos his hair? The way he chews his food, it's probably saying volumes of dialogue, you just need to figure it out. The communicating, it's been there all along, it just needs to be decoded. Yup, that's the ticket.

- **Good Bargaining:** The Shoe Sale at Nordstrom; Women's Consignment Shops on the Upper East Side; Halloween Decorations on November 1. Other than that, there is no good bargaining. No buyer's remorse here. It's happening, now let's keep moving on.

Stage 4: Depression

Sadness, only worse. Sadness that is insidious. Sadness that makes you not want to comb your hair in the morning because you just can't muster the energy and it wouldn't matter if you could—hair is the least of your problems. They have medicine for this now, don't you know? Know, too, that depression is going to cross over all of these different stages of grief. You can be in denial and also sad. Same goes for bargaining. So you're getting double-whammied, actually. You're a smart cookie, though, you know to expect depression. You've aligned yourself with a therapist or counselor who will help you get through the gloom and doom. Sure you have your girlfriends, but sometimes all of the kind words in the world won't make a bit of difference. Here's where the assistance of an expert is invaluable. Take advantage of it. I had session after session talking about my depression with my therapist. I told her about how I moped around on the weekends, how reading the ingredients on a cereal box would reduce me to a weepy mess. I told her all of it, and as I did, each depression event became easier and easier to overcome. Sharing these moments with a trusted friend or well-paid professional is critical to your divorce recovery, because when you retell those moments, they move to a more abstract space in your psyche. At some point—I know this is hard to imagine—these moments will seem like nonevents as you look back at them. You know that phrase, "getting it out of your system"? And I'm not just talking about the morning after a late night of vodka tonics and your three best girlfriends. I'm talking about getting those emotions out of you—literally releasing them. When you are depressed, those emotions need to be eliminated—even exorcised—from your being. So cry it out, and talk, talk, talk about your depression with your therapist. It will help you get through this stage; definitely one of the most overwhelming ones.

- **Bad Depression:** You absentmindedly flip through TV channels for hours until you finally find one showing a *Sleepless in Seattle* marathon. All of a sudden, a quiet evening watching mindless TV sets off a full-on bawl fest. You curl up in the fetal position and envision impaling yourself on the Space Needle. You're so depressed the next morning you call in sick to work. You stop wearing makeup, getting your clothes dry cleaned, and paying bills. This is bad. You have to know this is not healthy. Please call a professional and get help. And by professional, I don't mean High Priest Odysseus and his tarot card parlor above the falafel shop.
- **Good Depression:** You absentmindedly flip through TV channels for hours until you finally find one showing a *Sleepless in Seattle* marathon. All of a sudden, a quiet evening watching mindless TV sets off a full-on bawl fest. You pick up the phone and call an uber-friend, and in less than an hour your support system arrives in the form of a bag of cheese doodles (the light, puffy kind that leave your fin-

gers orange), your favorite red wine, and a beat-up copy of *The Breakfast Club.* Watching the movie prompts hysterical and embarrassing stories of high school and a perm that left you with chemical scars for sideburns. Before long, the tears are ones of laughter, and a potential depression downward spiral has been righted.

Stage 5: Acceptance

Woo hoo! How far you have come! The light at the end of the tunnel. The part of the journey where you are—can you believe it?—okay with what's happened. You've gone through every up and down, and a few corkscrews to boot. If you're reading this book for the first time, it's quite possible that you aren't there yet, but no worries, you will be at some point. Really. There's no good acceptance or bad acceptance per se, because once you're there, you've crossed the finish line. Wipe the sweat off your brow and stop huffing and puffing. You made it. I knew you would.

Not to deflate your happy balloon—because understand that you have made significant progress if you have reached acceptance—but acceptance is defined as having come to terms with what's happened, that you recognize it is part of your life. It doesn't necessarily mean you have found peace with it. It also doesn't automatically translate into life is great. You could still be angry about it, still may not be able to see the positive upside, and you may still carry around the voodoo doll of your ex that you occasionally poke with sewing needles.

There's another event—not grief related, but post-acceptance—that puts realization on the better parts of what you've been through, and is the lid on the acceptance jar. The completion of acceptance, if you will. That's not a stage of grief, but it is a sort of closure to the entire grieving process.

- **Bad Acceptance:** Accepting your new singlehood is a milestone not to be minimized. You are now part of a contingency of women who have endured similar pain and stress, and can breathe a sigh of relief (or let out a resounding "Yee Haw!"—depending on their style) that it's over and you've moved on to better things. If you came out of this with a greater financial windfall than your ex (in other words, you got the beach house and the sports car), this is not the time to gloat. As in sports, good sportsmanship applies here. Okay to spike the ball at the field-goal line; not okay to use your divorce-settlement windfall to buy a big message board at the home team's stadium that reads, "Hey, [ex's name here]: I am victorious, you piece of crap!" Decorum and maturity go a long way here. You are allowed to celebrate the end of your emotional journey, just don't make him feel bad because of it.
- **Good Acceptance:** You've made it; it's all good, baby! Celebrate and reward yourself accordingly. Once you've accepted your divorce, you can now take on new and exciting challenges that you want to take on, all on your own terms.

DIVORCED GIRLS' SOCIETY TENETS

✓ The five stages will affect you in your own personal way.

✓ Depression is part of the process, and will probably pack the biggest punch, and cross into the other four stages as well, tricky little emotion that it is.

✓ Therapy, therapy, therapy!

✓ It's okay to be angry—let it out, sister!

Mirror, Mirror on the Wall, Who's the Fairest of Them All: Learning to See Yourself Again

There was an immediate self-assessment that took place once my husband made his declaration. I started picking up the magnifying mirror more often, trying to identify what physical shortcoming did me in. My flaws seemed tenfold, and of course I couldn't help but wonder: Was it a varicose vein—the one right there—that became the catalyst to the end of my marriage? Or maybe the state of disarray my eyebrows continued to be in? I loved pampering as much as the next girl, but between a job, a child, and the thousands of other loose ends I tied up on a daily basis, weeks could go by before a trip to the salon bubbled to the top of my priorities. Half the time, even I didn't make the list of my top priorities.

So why, now that my marriage had fallen apart, was I thinking that a standing appointment with Raoul should have been number one on my to-do list?

Every morning I would think back to our day-to-day existence and how comfortable I had been without makeup, in the underwear with the loose elastic. A comfort that made me so . . . *uncomfortable* now. In an instant, I went from being blissfully unaware of how I looked to overly self-conscious about every little physical flaw, no matter how miniscule.

Like most women going through a divorce, I started to constantly second-guess the candid approach with which I revealed my physical flaws to my ex: *Was it a good idea, in retrospect, to have shown him how hairy my bikini line actually got before the wax appointment? Should I have explained in such detail the lower gastrointestinal manifestations that occurred after eating the company cafeteria's chicken chili? Why, oh why, did I point out that my left breast is slightly smaller than my right one?*

This went on for a few weeks, until one day I looked in the mirror and there was nothing left to criticize, no more flaws to place under the microscope and examine with the keen eye of a laboratory scientist. And that's when it occurred to me: While I was getting caught up in how my estranged husband may have seen me, I was forgetting to think about how *I* see me.

Snow White I Wasn't, but I Wasn't Exactly a Hook-Nosed Witch, Either

I was wasting so much energy trying to figure out how I didn't measure up physically, I couldn't recognize that, in the grand scheme of things, it just didn't matter. Did I have physical shortcomings? Of course I did! Everybody does. The thing is, the end of my marriage had nothing to do with how scary I looked with the terry-cloth turban on my head as I emerged from the shower each morning (that conclusion sounds like perfect common sense now, but it did take me a while to get there). We all look less than perfect in our day-to-day lives. Chances are your husband saw the good, the bad, and the ugly more times than you'd care to know. He probably wasn't expecting to find Pamela Anderson on the pillow next to him when he rolled over every morning (and if he was, there should be some perverse comfort in realizing that your partner was in fact a fourteen-year-old boy masquerading in a man's body). After all, what woman wouldn't want to wake up every morning and find Matthew McConaughey gazing back at her crusty eyes? Was your husband even in the same league as Matthew? Even close? Didn't think so.

Here I was taking on the full burden of the situation, performing the daily self-assessments and physical evaluations that could only lead to pulling the sheets over my head and hoping that another human being would never be forced to share the bed with my hammer toe. But I wasn't the only one in this relationship. So why was I beating myself up for being less than a perfect physical specimen?

Maybe the idea of being perfect fell down on your list of priorities, too, as you and your partner grew more comfortable together. In the early stages, you may have worked a bit harder to be that perfect ten. Plucking your eyebrows religiously, bikini waxes every three weeks. Admit it, though, the longer you were together, the more comfortable things became. You went from full made-up face to glasses and hair pulled back in a terrycloth headband in three short months. And for good reason: The match was made, you guys were getting along like peas and carrots, and you were able to let your perfect self slide just a bit. The highlight appointments that should have been every four weeks grew to every eight, and what was the harm in letting out an occasional burp? Within six months you were belching the ABCs better than your six-year-old nephew (and could get to "L," where he had run out of breath at "H"), and abandoned the concept of shutting the door while sitting on the toilet.

But then the announcement is made and the relationship is on its way to being over. And for some reason, the comfort level reverts to pre-dating days. It's different, awkward, and sets off a host of weird inner dialogue. And that's when you start to freak out about every little physical detail. You don't want him to see you in your jammies, and you've stopped playing the pull-my-finger game. In this new world, it's hard not to have a heightened sensitivity to your physical self when the person who has seen every part of you is now, not at all, a part of your life. The whys invariably turn to your body, hair, face, and teeth. The physical self is easy to latch on to, because it stares you in the face each and every day. Plus you feel some semblance of control and responsibility over it, since every gel, cream, mousse, and elixir exists to plump, reduce, shine, or smooth.

So when you break out the magnifying mirror—you know, the one with the stage makeup lights built in—and stare at the lines, the blotches, the uneven brows, it's hard not to be critical. But, we're not here to deconstruct what specific physical trait may have driven you apart.

Because really, it doesn't matter. Where would it get you if you knew? Besides, there's a pretty good chance it wasn't some random physical flaw—if it was, then good riddance, how could you have lasted this long with such a shallow cad?

No, I was going about it all wrong. What I needed to do was point the mirror in the other direction: at him.

> ## MANTRAS to get you through the day
>
> *I can rock a miniskirt!*

And You Can Bet He Is No Prince

For some reason, I figured my husband had to believe he was somehow better than me—that he could do better than me. Why else would he choose to leave? But you know what made it better, what made it easier to turn a blind eye to the whitehead festering on my tear-stained cheek? I turned my newly honed attention to detail on him.

Here's a chance for you to leverage your observational skills and start to get your confidence back. His ears? Remember that elementary-school nickname he told you in confidence? Dumbo? Yeah, now you can see why. Whereas before you gave his physical shortcomings the benefit of the doubt, now it's safe to notice them. In fact, I'd highly recommend it.

Is this you being petty? I don't think so. I wasn't making my observations out loud, nor was I sharing my pet peeves with others. Instead I used them to give myself a level playing field, even if it was just in my own head.

So, go ahead and remind yourself of all of the things he did to trigger your gag reflex. Does he smell his socks before tossing them in the hamper? Does he pick his nose and then examine the fruits of his labor? Are there unsightly hairs emerging from unlikely places—nose, ears, back? Maybe it's his feet.

Believe me, it's easier than you'd think. Flaws and annoying habits are everywhere once you decide to pay attention. But don't spend too much time gloating over the fact that he actually has more hair on his ass than you do on your entire body. Because you've got a life to live, and there's no time like the present.

The real lesson here is that trying to find an answer in the flab hanging from your arm isn't going to change anything. There will be no a-ha moment when you discover the mole that did you in. Accepting yourself is the first step toward accepting the reality of your situation. And one of the true blessings of an otherwise-shitty situation is the chance to, silently, start seeing yourself—and him—through realistic eyes.

And me? I saw that I had it all going on. Sure, I still looked a little goofy in the terry turban, still had the same barely-B-cup boobs, and still fretted over uneven skin. But that almost made me feel better, believe it or not. I was still the same person—a person I liked being, even if I was about to go it alone. At thirty-eight years old, I was comfortable with myself, and that was one thing I didn't want to change.

So that's when I put the mirror away and stopped worrying how my husband saw me, and started figuring out who I wanted to see when I looked in the mirror (but I did get those eyebrows cleaned up—that was $12 well spent).

What Your GIRLFRIEND *Is Thinking*

Look at all she's doing! Dare I say that I'm feeling a wee bit envious hearing about all of her new plans: trips to Europe, a weekend in Hilton Head by herself (yes, *herself!*), new classes and opportunities to try things she always wanted to do. She even gets, *gulp*, some time away from her kid without the guilt that usually hangs over me when I squeeze in a Saturday manicure.

Wait a minute—she's starting to make divorce look like fun. Yes, it sounds ridiculous. And I know it's crazy. But all of a sudden her world seems to be opening up, and my staid little world feels like it's closing in around me.

It may be a bit irrational—jealous of a friend whose marriage was ripped apart? No way! But jealous of a friend who gets to start over, to have the freedom and the wisdom (something we didn't have way back when we had the freedom) to pursue her wildest dreams? Absolutely.

Be Adventurous: Taking a Bite out of the Apple

Once my crisis of self-esteem had settled down from a full-on boil to a simmer (unfortunately, it never goes away completely), it was time to move on—beyond the what was it about me?s to the what about me?

In my case, as the weekends played out, I realized that my life couldn't stop just because my marriage was over. No, you can't play a game of tennis by yourself, and it really does take two to tango, but I didn't want to stop doing what I enjoyed. It would only make the newly created void in my life (my ex) seem like a huge gaping hole. The challenging part, however, was learning how to do "it" alone. And the "it" may also be something you haven't even figured out yet. If you've always loved painting, or marathon running, or other solitary pastimes (including a good game of solitaire), more power to you. But the ones that require you to pair up also require an added boost of confidence to start doing again.

I quickly discovered that rediscovering what you enjoy is easier if you follow a few basic guidelines:

Get Your Friends Involved

Friends can be great stand-ins or temporary replacements, a buffer zone if you will, if you're not quite ready to venture out alone. Who wouldn't love an offer to hit the clay courts for a set or two (followed by a round of drinks bought by the loser)? That's what friends are for, even if their backstroke could use a little work. Sure, you have to pick up the phone and risk sounding desperate for the company, but friends won't care. And good friends will be thrilled to see you interested in diversions and hobbies (voodoo-doll making and secret witch-potion brewing notwithstanding), and will enthusiastically join in. In fact, they may even suggest you schedule a regular weekly game.

Need help? Try this exercise.

Make two lists for yourself. The first list can give you a good idea of what you can immediately take on if you're ready to try something new, but want a sort of safety zone. The second list is more of a stretch, but may also give you a greater sense of accomplishment.

One should be a list of things you like to do, and already know how to do—don't worry about how meaningful these things are: singing, gardening, walking your dog.

_____

_____

_____

_____

_____

The other should be a list of things you want to learn or wish you knew how to do: tap dancing, getting your MBA, making sushi, learning Italian.

_____

_____

_____

_____

_____

Now that you've identified some activities that you can do now and those you'd like to pursue, write down the names of some friends and the activities you would enjoy doing together; then pick up the phone and make a date. Remember, there's no such thing as an activity that's too small (browsing in a bookstore); in fact, it's the easiest place to start.

Friend   **Activity**

_____

_____

_____

_____

_____

When Going Solo, Start Small

So you've always loved to travel, but a solo trip to the Amazon rainforests seems a little daunting when the idea of venturing beyond a 5-mile radius of your house paralyzes you with fear. The lesson here is not to bite off more than you can chew. There is plenty of time for globe-trotting in the future. Right now it isn't about grand gestures, but about reconnecting with yourself and the things you enjoy. Start small and remember why you loved doing certain things and why you deserve to do what brings you joy. Then work your way up. The Amazon will still be there in a year.

Need some help? Try this exercise:

Write down some activities you used to enjoy but haven't found the time for lately:

Activity	Why It Brings Me Joy

Now, write down some activities you enjoy, or used to enjoy, and would like to try again. Then make a date with yourself and do it!

Activity	Start Date

I decided to start *very small*. I went out to eat.

As a soon-to-be single woman, a trendy downtown restaurant that once sounded appealing was now fiercely intimidating. Nevertheless, I knew I had to start living my life, doing what I liked to do, and eating fabulous food was something that remained high on my list. I also looked at this as a positive learning opportunity for my daughter. Behaving well in a restaurant is a skill that always needs reinforcement for little ones. So, with my adventurous four-year-old in tow, we went downtown to try a new French bistro.

MANTRAS to get you through the day

*I have a chance to discover what
I enjoy—and rediscover who
I am in the process.*

It was the talk of the town. I wore my favorite jean skirt, thankful that my new running habit had actually turned my legs into something more appealing than the miniature tree trunks I had grown used to. But when we walked into the restaurant, I panicked. Reminding myself why it seemed like a great idea earlier in the day didn't really help: So what if my daughter never learned to eat a dinner that didn't come in a Happy Meal box? So what if I lived on Lean Cuisine and frozen pizza for a few years? As we stood in front of the maître d's podium, I wondered, *What the hell was I thinking?*

Were the patrons staring at me in my jean skirt that all of a sudden seemed too short for my thirty-something legs? Were those dirty looks coming from the kind of people who don't like kids dining anywhere near them? Or was that just me playing paranoid single gal?

So often we are convinced that the whole world can see our flaws and our insecurities, but the truth is, they don't. Not only does it not matter, they probably aren't thinking anything about you or what you perceive to be your physical quirks. You're not a Hollywood headliner; the rest of the world isn't checking you out. Now go get on with your life.

Our dinner experience was great. As an older couple left our section of the restaurant, the woman leaned in and whispered, "I so admire you." I wasn't sure if she was referring to the fact that I was a single mom bringing her child out to eat, or worse, that I dared to sport such a short skirt. Regardless, I was flattered that someone admired me, in a restaurant where I was earlier convinced that everyone was appalled by the sight of me and my little companion.

I knew I'd taken one step, albeit a baby step, in the right direction. And that went a long way to helping me see that I could still enjoy the things that made me happy, even though I wasn't married. Plus, my daughter never eats all her fries. This successful field trip gave me the courage to embark on another eating extravaganza, this time sans child, at my favorite Thai place. Just me and my goong gah tiem, proving to myself that I was able to dine alone without feeling judged. And the sweat on my brow? That would be from the chili peppers—honest.

Tips for Your SPEED-DIAL SISTERS

You don't need a life-altering divorce to remember you've always wanted to sit behind a potter's wheel or sketch a hot guy in the nude. Remember when you envied your newly single friend those tai chi lessons she signed up for? Always envisioned yourself a martial arts master? Well, here's your chance. Your friend might really enjoy sharing her new love of all things yoga with you. This is truly an opportunity for some give and take between a Speed-Dial Sister and her divorcing friend.

While you may not have a degree on the wall that suggests you'd make a stellar career or life counselor, there are small things you can do to help enable your newly single friend's journey. Are you volunteering? No? Well, my dear, maybe a few hours a month at the women's shelter (with the girlfriend who now needs those kinds of distractions) is exactly the motivation you need. Or maybe you're already organizing the breast cancer relay. Don't forget to include your divorcing friend. She needs those kinds of events and efforts to focus on, to help her get through her divorce. You may both find that dedicating a few hours a month to something can be extremely gratifying, and may actually make you both feel great.

But as wonderful as all this togetherness may seem, there are some pitfalls to avoid. Your friend needs to find what *she* loves to do, the activities that bring *her* joy. Swimming the backstroke at 6:00 A.M. may be your idea of nirvana, but if your invitation is declined and your gift of new goggles returned, don't take it personally. Keep doing those laps, just don't be hurt that your friend isn't playing Marco Polo next to you.

And even if you've both discovered your inner sailors after years of promising to do so, don't forget to give your friend her space. Part of the process of discovering what she enjoys is rediscovering who she is. If you're always there reminding her to hoist the jib, that kind of defeats the purpose. As much as you're both enjoying the opportunity to yell "Ahoy, ye matey" across the bow, don't forget to give your friend her space every once in a while, too.

Hi Ho, Hi Ho . . . Deciding Where You Want to Go

If you've already perfected the art of dining out solo, you may want to spread those wings a bit further now, and explore other diversions that force you to interact with others. Pick situations where you can't hide behind a paperback or focus all of your concentration on cutting up your daughter's chicken cutlet.

While your criteria for picking the activity should include whether it brings you joy, it doesn't have to include the possibility of meeting a next significant other, although that would be an awfully nice ancillary benefit. This is simply an opportunity for you to think about yourself and what you like to do. There was certainly no chance of meeting Mr. Right when I chose my second activity—an all-women a cappella singing group. It was perfect for me, and not because I have a voice like Whitney Houston. No, I'd just always wanted an excuse to sing.

I discovered the group on a bulletin board at work and immediately knew I wanted to give it a try. And a teeny, tiny part of me acknowledged that I never would have thought of spending my Tuesday nights in a church basement with twenty altos and sopranos (and even a few baritones) while married. But now, with a few spare nights a week thanks to joint-custody arrangements, I now had the time—and no one to justify it to—to take on things I hadn't before. This just felt absolutely right at the time, for a few reasons. For one, it was very non-threatening, since there were only women involved. And second, it had the right level of intensity, where I knew I was committing to something that I could direct my energies (and musical talents) toward. It was exactly what I wanted to do with my free time, a great learning experience, and free! So I donned my pitch pipe and auditioned for the chorus. There was absolutely no chance in hell of meeting a Mr. Right while doo-wopping with a group of middle-aged music teachers, but it reminded me of what I was passionate about. Those three hours I spend each Tuesday night are ones I eagerly look forward to. Nothing but singing, just me and my best Aretha Franklin impersonation. And best of all, I'm too busy trying to read the notes on the sheet to worry about lawyers, broken hearts, and what life has in store for me.

There are so many choices available, and they don't all have to fulfill a deep-seated childhood fantasy of dancing the *Nutcracker* or starting your own jam and preserves business. Maybe you simply decide to volunteer. Often, focusing on others helps to remind us that life does go on, and that we actually don't have it so bad. It can also make you feel like you're making a difference, and when you're in a situation that seems so out of your control, being able to actually have an impact somewhere can be pretty damn nice.

I've tried a few volunteering opportunities, and have found some more palatable than others. I spent one July afternoon building a house, and soon realized, after smacking my left thumb with a hammer one too many times, that I wasn't exactly at risk of being recruited into the United Brotherhood of Carpenters. It was then, too, that I finally understood what people meant when they talked about the oppressive Richmond humidity in summer. Passing out programs at the local symphony's Christmas concert was definitely more my speed. Though if you're more interested in meeting men and can tolerate physical labor, building houses definitely shows more promise. The symphony? Well, if you don't mind men with hearing aids and colostomy bags. . . . Determine what your volunteer goals are, and then find the most appropriate volunteer programs.

If you're unsure of where to even begin, try the following exercise.

Write down some issues or subjects that really strike a chord with you (animals, children, women, the arts). Then research organizations that address these areas, and offer your help.

Issue/Subject   **Organization/Contact Info**

_____

_____

_____

_____

_____

Go Ahead and Make Your Declaration of Independence

I got a cat. Just like that. Meow.

It was one of the first big decisions I made as a newly single person. Yes, my ex-husband was allergic to cats, but no, that wasn't the primary driver here. I really just wanted a cat. I always have. And for the first time, there was nothing stopping me from driving down to the shelter and picking one out. His name is Wolfie, and he's blind in one eye, but the moment he walked through our front door, he felt like family. And even though there's now a litter box to clean, and a few cat hairs on the couch, when Wolfie jumps on my lap looking for a snuggle, I don't regret the decision for a single minute.

My therapist even recommended that I include the cat in my annual Christmas picture, announcing the newest member of my family. I didn't do that. No, didn't want the rest of the world to think I had become a freaky cat lady so recently after the end of my marriage. (Save that for thirty years down the road, when it might not seem so crazy to have a small Victorian home in rural New England, complete with lace doilies on all of the side tables, and the requisite house full of cats. Okay, that still seems crazy.) But my therapist's point was to encourage me to view this as a celebration of sorts, to acknowledge the big deal that it was, and let the rest of the world know that life was moving on for me.

Another thing I did, however small, was get a vanity license plate with my maiden name on it. It was this totally innocuous act, but so deeply symbolic for me. It was my own way to very publicly announce to the world that I was my own person. But I don't anticipate changing my last name anytime soon—not when my maiden name includes twelve consonants and an umlaut.

One Small Step for Womankind, One Giant Step for You!

- Get a vanity license plate.
- Go back to using your maiden name.
- Join a health club, book club, knitting circle, or any other group that shares your interests.
- Get rid of things you don't like in your house (couple of qualifiers, though: Make sure that either it belongs to you or that he and you have agreed that the item isn't a keeper. Don't worry if removing an item empties out a room . . . if you always hated that BarcaLounger in the den, pitch it. And as tempting as it may sound, make sure he's not in the BarcaLounger when you pitch it).

So you start small with things like dining out and maybe getting back into the swing of things on the tennis court, and then work your way up. As I said, this is about baby steps. When you are making those baby steps with ease and aplomb, start thinking bigger. Long-term plans. Activities you want to pursue, things that may seem daunting and out of reach today. You can start researching them now, so when you are ready to try the different, maybe somewhat intimidating new thing, you know where to sign up. Friends and Speed-Dial Sisters are critical to your success here, because they can participate as well, and relieve some of the anxiety you may feel if you're doing things alone. It doesn't matter what it is. It's a time to experiment, be kind to yourself, and rediscover what brings you joy.

DIVORCED GIRLS' SOCIETY TENETS

✓ Cellulite on the thighs and a big nose are immaterial. Put down the mirror and concentrate on the thing that does matter: your life.

✓ Step out. Even if it's just baby-steps out. A new coffeehouse, that paint-your-own-pottery place you've always wanted to try? Get out there and enjoy your town.

✓ Interests make you interesting. So set down on paper some thoughts on the kinds of interests you want to pursue—no matter how small.

✓ Make a declaration to yourself, something that is small but meaningful. Something like a necklace with a simple charm that has significance to you (like a globe, because you plan on traveling, or the initials of those important in your life—like your children).

The First Holiday, or How Not to Cry at the Sight of Pumpkin Pie

I know what you're thinking: The idea of celebrating anything—Christmas, Valentine's Day, even Arbor Day—elicits an eye roll and a groan. It's completely in conflict with the emotions you are feeling these days. So much so, that you wish for all holidays to be called off for the year, if not longer. Unfortunately, and as much as your friends need to continually remind you of this, the world does not revolve around you. And as surely as the sun comes up each morning, so too, do Thanksgiving, New Year's Eve, and Memorial Day weekends.

Holidays take preparation. They require a plan. So you've convinced yourself that Valentine's Day will roll off your back like a dark-chocolate truffle with cocoa powder? Think again. One glimpse of those formerly tacky candy-heart lollipops on a stick (you know, the ones with complimentary white teddy bear attached), and your willpower will melt faster than that Hershey's Kiss you've been carrying around in your pocket for two weeks. There are at least ten noteworthy holidays on the calendar, and most should cause you no concern. Flag Day will come and go and you're none the worse for the wear. Columbus Day? You're the woman of steel. Martin Luther King Jr. Day? You demonstrate greater resolve than Rosa Parks. But the big ones—Christmas, Passover, birthdays—can pack an emotional punch that makes a Mike Tyson ear munch seem like harmless child's play.

Dust Off Those Blinking Christmas-Tree Earrings: It's Time to Enjoy the Holidays Again

As it is with many big life changes, sometimes it's best to start small. Picking one or two holidays to focus on can help you get back into the holiday groove. In other words, don't start with Christmas. Unless, of course, you're reading this and it's December 20. In which case, I recommend calling up a Speed-Dial Sister and strategizing with her. Pronto. If you do have more time to plan, you might want to pick, say, July 4. If you historically spent Independence Day at the beach with your ex-in-laws, go to the other extreme: the mountains! Do some research and pick a lovely town that celebrates the birth of our country with gusto—parade down Main Street, fire engine rides, seventeen-gun salute—the whole shebang. Enjoy the outdoor activities and cooler weather (your ex-mother-in-law never did crank the A/C high enough, good riddance to that little sweat box by the ocean). Or maybe you want to reclaim the beach for yourself. Was the Jersey Shore really your idea of sandy nirvana? Or was there a Cape Cod girl inside you waiting to burst out? Here's your chance to plant that striped umbrella in the sand and declare your sacred ground.

Or maybe you don't even have to hit the road. Find out where the closest fireworks display will be taking place and call a girlfriend to meet you, or just pack up the kids and make it a family event. Bring a picnic (don't forget the wine) and enjoy spending the holiday close to home. You may see some of those neighbors who were apprised of your situation, and they'll probably be impressed with your adventurous spirit. Not that you care about what others think. Really, your first holiday can be as big or small as you want. The key here is realizing that what some may call "tradition" others simply call "routine." Break out of it, and start your own.

Old Tradition	New Tradition
Superbowl Sunday	Take the kids sledding
Your wedding anniversary	Spa day with girlfriends
The day you met your ex	Sky-diving trip
New Year's skiing	New Year's skiing— with friends

The Divorced Girls' Society
GOLDEN RULES

- Do consider celebrating days that may not normally qualify as events worthy of storewide sales and boxes of decorations. The day you could finally talk about the end of your marriage without hyperventilating into fitful sobs? When you could finally discuss it in an abstract way, almost as if you were telling the story of another couple? That, my friend, is a day you must remember. Because it means you have now crossed over to the other side.

- Do pay even closer attention to important days occurring in the lives of your loved ones, and milk those for all they're worth. Your favorite niece just won the spelling bee? Sounds like a party to me! By noticing and acknowledging the special days of others, it'll help you get back into the festive mood, and realize that even though holidays with you-know-who are not going to happen anymore, there's still many important occasions to clink glasses to and wear silly hats for.

- Do invite others to celebrate with you—who doesn't like an excuse to break out the good crystal for a toast or ask the waiter if he can put a candle in that flourless chocolate cake?

- Don't be a curmudgeon. If there's absolutely nothing that can cheer you up during the holidays, at least don't drag everyone else down into your gloom pit. So, while the last thing you may feel like doing is leading the fa-la-las around the piano at Christmastime, it's not okay to sigh in exasperation or roll your eyes when the family asks for everyone's participation for another round of "Jingle Bells." Your family wants you to be happy—at least don't make them feel bad for trying to make you feel better. If it's unbearable, then call it a night. You do have your Get-Out-of-Jail-Free Cards, but like I've said before, they don't give you license to be a raging bitch. At least not all the time.

- Don't dwell on special days that are no longer special. Your wedding anniversary: Now, it's just an ordinary day. Don't treat it any differently than the day before. In other words, not a good idea to watch your wedding video or see if your wedding dress still fits.

There's No Hallmark Card to Buy, But It's Still Worth Celebrating

The thing about holidays is that they aren't perfect; not even the big ones. It's common knowledge that Jesus wasn't actually born on December 25. But people were already celebrating something around the third week of December—the solstice. So in an effort to promote Christianity, the Romans decided to work both angles, appease the pagans and promote Jesus by putting his birthday closer to the solstice. And the tree? Pagan.

Throughout history, holidays have been manipulated, fabricated, and reinvented—Sweetest Day, anyone? You, too, can take that time-honored approach to the momentous days in your own personal history. There's no holiday police—you won't get a knock on your door if you decide that there's a new holiday called "The Day I Realized It's More Fun to Play in a Tennis League than Watch Fly-Fishing on ESPN." Consider setting aside a day for

something that commemorates your non-married life—
the day you took back your maiden name, the day you
opened up your checking account as a single gal. Break
out the streamers and confetti. Play a little Kool and the
Gang and celebrate.

Why Families and Holidays Can't Be Separated or, There's a Reason You Can't Buy a One-Pound Turkey Roaster

For whatever reason, the holidays are inexorably linked
to families. You can't think of one without the other, particularly when you think of the big three, the veritable
grand slam: Christmas, Thanksgiving, and Easter, for
the Christians among us; and Passover, Rosh Hoshana,
and Thanksgiving for others. Your current situation can
create an added level of stress to the already nausea-
inducing nervousness of getting through the holidays.
Some women may fear their families won't display the
kid-glove mentality needed during this trying time. Add
to that the extended family members who may not have
been born with the sensitivity gene, and those who are
simply clueless, while you are teetering on the brink of
straitjacket city. There will always be the cousin who,
after reaching for the bowl of mashed potatoes will ask,
"So when did you fall out of love with your husband
and decide to ditch your family?" or "How long was he
having sex with his secretary before you found out?"
Yeah, it's dumb. Sure, this person is demonstrating less
common sense than that bowl of potatoes. So roll with
it. Graciously pass those potatoes and tell him, "Long
enough to catch a raging case of crabs."

Tips for Your SPEED-DIAL SISTERS

You can't buy your divorcing friend love, but you can treat her like a queen.

It never occurred to me that a silly little nightshirt would have such an impact. I was Christmas shopping in a local boutique and noticed a stack of nightshirts with cute sayings about friends. The shirt with a bottle of wine caught my attention because Vicki's a huge fan of wine. When I read the saying across the front—*Like a good bottle of wine, friends get better with age*—I knew I had to get it. So I popped it in the mail the next day. When Vicki called to say she'd received it, I could hear her choke up. The woman was actually crying! *Why on earth was this little nightshirt such a big deal?* The fact is, Vicki wasn't getting many unexpected and fun surprises. So this was perfect. It probably wouldn't have mattered what I sent. Just the fact that I was thinking about her is what really mattered. I wanted to show Vicki that I cared. I wanted her to know she wasn't alone.

It's easy for your divorcing friend to get irrational right now and think that she is utterly unlovable. Of course, nothing could be further from the truth, and this is when friends can help. Even little things can have a big effect. A book she might enjoy, a CD of some new singer she'd love to croon along with, even a postcard. Women going through divorce sometimes feel they are on a sinking ship all alone. Life preservers, in the form of a small gift or letter, are warm and comforting reminders that your friend is still loved. And that means a lot when she's not feeling the love at home.

My first Christmas I tried to be smart. I stuck to a small gathering (sensing a theme here?), inviting only family to my house, my turf. Our holiday was decidedly less formal than usual, but I still did my best to make it comfortable. I didn't decide to bail on the holiday cheer by ditching the turkey, and instead tossing a pan of Stouffer's macaroni and cheese on the table and yelling, "Eat up!" Admittedly, though, I was feeling particularly raw and wounded when the holidays rolled around a mere seven weeks after the big news. I prepared myself for a totally wretched experience. An endless and painful day during which the turkey mocked me, the stuffing reminded me of lost family traditions, and the gravy was lumpy. I steeled myself for the empty seat at the table where a conspicuously absent family member would usually sit, braced myself for the awkward silences from family members who didn't know how to act.

MANTRAS to get you through the day

Valentine's Day: J eschew you!

What I found was just the opposite. Families can be great, loving, supportive units. And they will bend over backwards to help you forget what you're going through and focus on the here and now.

If this doesn't hold true for you, and your extended family turns out to be the real-life version of Carol Burnett's Eunice and Mama, you do have some recourse. A polite nudge in the right direction in the form of, "I'd like the family to be the focus today; let's not talk about me," sets the tone nicely without making you seem defensive. Maybe some people won't get the hint. That's when you take your Get-Out-of-Jail-Free Cards in hand and respond with a curt, "I don't think the holidays are the right time to discuss my personal life, thanks" if nosy Uncle Henry starts asking if you think your ex might be gay or on his way to rehab.

Consider cutting your family get-together short if it becomes an unbearable event, and you can no longer tolerate the odd stares and inappropriate lines of questioning. Or maybe you're just not up for all of the cheeriness when the best part of the night so far has been the rum you added to your eggnog. A simple, "I'd love to stay for dessert, but I've made another commitment that I must get to," will do. No one needs to know that the other commitment means getting home early, getting the kids in their jammies, and having a slumber party in your bed, complete with pumpkin pie and the movie *Home Alone*.

Remember also, you can actually alert a few influential family members to the fact that you just don't want to talk about the big change in your life during the big get-togethers. Invoke the No-Fly Zone with the right people, and they'll most likely pass the word around to others.

I had visions of a clueless relative announcing just before the turkey carving, "Why don't we go around the table and say what we're grateful for?" To which I would have been reduced to a sniveling, blithering mess as I came to the erroneous conclusion that there was very little to be thankful for, but lots to want to cry about. We didn't go around the table that year, but a relative did raise her wine glass and say a wonderful prayer and thanks to our family. I realized that life goes on, the family will always be the family no matter what state my marital status is in, and I clinked my glass with everyone else's.

And a Few Other Occasions . . .

Beyond the traditional holidays, there are also some memorable dates in your life now that don't exactly merit the little gold star on your refrigerator calendar: the day you met your ex, the day you said I Do, and the not-so celebratory day you and your husband went your separate ways. While you can't make those moments in your life go away, you can make a point of not letting them get the best of you. In time, you'll be able to face them without the big, messy emotions attached. For a change, maybe schedule your first barium enema appointment on the day of your wedding anniversary. Or, consider ordering one of those green dumpsters to be delivered to your house each year on the day your ex moved out. Consider it a metaphor for a purged life.

Holiday-Tradition Redux

Halloween: Was your former spouse a stickler about giving out candy? Did he buy the Dum Dums when everyone knows kids want the one-pound Hershey bars? Go big for Halloween—you'll be known as the house with the cool lady who gives out full-sized bags of Skittles. You'll get even more props from the local kids if you don the plastic green teeth and the giant pointed hat.

Christmas: Did you always want that giant, six-foot plastic snow globe, the one that's hooked up to a generator and kicks up Styrofoam snowflakes while a Santa waves at passersby? Do it. So what if your neighborhood association leaves a threatening letter in your mailbox. Make Christmas your own. Dial it up or down as you prefer. If your ex turned your house into a Macy's parade and you prefer a flickering candle in each window, then this year, make your house festive on your terms. And your holiday card? This is where you can really demonstrate your new status, in a very deliberate, customized way. Consider the alternative card choices: a murky watercolor of a horse and carriage clomping through a snowy Vermont town, or a picture of you running your first 10K race, your hands raised in victory. No, it's not religious. And does the rest of the world really want to see you in all of your sweaty, neoprene-wearing glory? Probably not, but it's *your* holiday card. And that's what matters.

Valentine's Day: It has the power to render a single gal feeling hopeless, unloved, and angry at the world. Everywhere she turns, heart-shaped boxes of chocolate appear to be laughing at her; cheap roses in their self-contained vials of water shake their collective crimson petals and seem to mutter "tsk, tsk." But this holiday is about LOVE, and surely you love many people: your children, mom, dad, sister and brother, grandmother. And let's not forget girlfriends. Send flowers to your grandmother—won't she find that unexpected? Your best girlfriend loves those pedicures where they wrap your legs in seaweed, so how about getting her a gift certificate for an afternoon of playing *Sigmund and the Sea Monster?*

Birthdays: If you've always celebrated your birthday like a rock star, then there's no reason to stop. But if you've typically kept the festivities humdrum, then consider this a holiday you may want to play up a bit more than you did in the past. Remember, Demi Moore has turned forty into the new thirty; getting older is getting easier, and the stigmas are disappearing. So what's to stop you from celebrating that next year with a little more oomph? And maybe it's not even a public celebration. Earmark $100 for you to do with whatever you want, no justification required—a massage and facial at the downtown spa, a new handbag in a totally impractical color, or loading up the freezer with your favorite cut of steak. It's your call.

If you have kids, consider focusing your celebratory prowess on a blowout for your ten-year-old that will keep everyone at Filmore Elementary School buzzing for weeks.

DIVORCED GIRLS' SOCIETY TENETS

✓ Make up your own holidays: the invention of the appletini? That day should be immortalized in history. If nothing else, the beverage you serve at that celebration is clearly a no-brainer.

✓ Own your holidays—they now belong to you. No need to fight over white versus colored lights. Do it up the way you like it.

✓ Be prepared for those rude family members who make Nurse Ratched seem sensitive and caring. At holiday gatherings, remove yourself from situations that are making you ill, or pull out a Get-Out-of-Jail-Free Card and cut them off when you've had it.

✓ When attending family gatherings, identify and then stick close to extended family members who actually do have a sensitivity chip in their emotional circuit board.

When You're Blubbering Like a Baby, but There's Another Child in the House

You know those little creatures who eat you out of house and home? The ones who, when they get a nosebleed, run through the entire upstairs screaming for you, leaving a bloody trail befitting a Stephen King movie on your white carpet? The ones who beg and plead for you to make them a quesadilla with the George Foreman grill, and then eat only one bite, after you've smacked yourself in the head while pulling it off of the high cabinet shelf, tore apart the kitchen looking for the directions on how to use it, and burned your fingers twice? Yes, those little gems. As if you didn't already have enough stresses in your life managing this strange new world called divorce, you might also have the added bonus of little people.

A part of you probably wishes you could temporarily place your children in a time machine, and drop them directly into the future when all this messy divorce stuff has been worked out and you are living your new (and improved) lives as divorced mom and dad. Hell, you probably wish there was room in that time machine for you, too.

MANTRAS to get you through the day

Mothers are not invincible, but they are in charge.

But while we await the realization of the aforementioned *Star Trek* fantasy, it's best we operate as if it's not going to happen anytime soon and set out a plan, or at least some considerations, to help you manage this life event with your children. Now, before you imagine a scene reminiscent of a cranky three-year-old in the cookie aisle, don't worry. It's not as bad as you think it will be; you just need to keep your perspective. And if you can manage through this part of it, consider yourself a stellar mom, parent, and all-around awesome human being. Yes, the presence of children adds a whole new dimension to this mess, but kids can also provide a much-needed source of humor (however unintentional)—plus, kids can also be a terrific source of strength. Not strength as in making your five-year-old carry the twenty-five-pound bag of cat litter you used to ask your ex to haul, but strength in the internal sense. When they look at you with their innocent little faces and declare their love for you when you're feeling quite unloved. That can keep your proverbial chin up on the worst of days.

Three Simple Rules (Okay, Maybe Not so Simple, but Definitely Helpful)

Since it's your job to see to it that everyone gets through this intact, here are three simple rules to keep in mind if little ones are part of your divorce.

Rule #1: Compartmentalize

Normally, the ability to compartmentalize your life might be looked down upon. Some may even argue it's unhealthy. And under any other circumstance, they may be right (or they could just be self-righteous prigs who aren't capable of such a sophisticated mental sorting system). But in any case, now is the time to think of yourself as a human wall of cubbies, with organized sections into which you can place different areas of your life. When your boss tells you that you need to develop your influencing skills, you recognize that she's giving you a work challenge; you don't start second-guessing how influential you are (or aren't) when buying a book of stamps from the clerk at the post office. You keep work issues in the work cubby. Same goes for parenting issues. Keep them separate from your ex-husband issues. This may sound easy enough, but it can be particularly difficult to do while you're jockeying between figuring out how to get *out* of each other's lives and discussing the one thing that keeps you *in* each other's lives—your kids.

If it helps, you could also think of parenting as analogous to running a business. The long-term objective is to raise well-adjusted, productive contributors to our society. (And before you wonder if Jeffrey Dahmer or Jack the Ripper came from divorced families, best not Google that fact, and instead check out "Children of Divorced Parents Who Went on to Do Great Things," opposite.) So while my ex and I battled it out over who got what, we both understood that was our problem, not our daughter's. And as such, we were able to shift gears and discuss—calmly and politely—our daughter's spring-break plans, or who was buying what for Christmas. It made us both seem somewhat bipolar, but if you can effectively compartmentalize, or view this as a business dealing rather than an emotional tug of war, you can succeed.

Your therapist has probably already told you that divorce doesn't screw up children. Nope. Parents that stop being parents—that's what turns little Joey into the playground thug. And when you consider the fact that divorce can be so emotionally taxing, so intensely overwhelming, a parent could, conceivably, stop parenting because they are so caught up in their own drama. So, repeat after me: "Just keep being a parent." The rules and routines should stay the same, to the extent that they can. Operate as if little has changed in terms of how mommy and daddy parent, even though the logistics may be slightly different.

Your children don't care about what you and your ex are battling over. My ex and I each hired two real estate experts, went three rounds of negotiations, and still ended up going to court because we couldn't agree on the market value of a small piece of beach property we owned together. It was a big deal to both of us, but meaningless to our daughter. Children just want their mom and dad. So even if the thought of sitting next to your ex at Junior's tae kwon do competition gives you an uncontrollable urge to karate chop him right in the nunchucks, know that Junior needs you both there, and that means more to him than the fact that you two are not married anymore. Keep it separate.

Children of Divorced Parents Who Went on to Do Great Things

Here's proof that divorce doesn't do irreparable harm to kids.

Presidents and Vice Presidents:
Bill Clinton, Gerald Ford, Dan Quayle

Wives of Presidents:
Nancy Reagan, Jackie Kennedy Onassis

Writers:
Dr. William Sears, Sinclair Lewis

Musicians:
Stephen Sondheim, John Lennon

Entertainment:
Al Pacino, Oprah Winfrey, Stephen Spielberg

Other Historical and Political Figures:
Booker T. Washington, Barack Obama, Steve Jobs

What Your GIRLFRIEND Is Thinking

The first time I was alone with Vicki's daughter, I thought I should acknowledge what was going on. I'd let her know that if she ever wanted to talk, she could talk to me. I wanted her to know that even though her parents were divorcing, there were plenty of people who loved her.

"You know that we all love you, right?" I asked her, choking up at the thought that this little girl probably felt like she was all alone, that her family was disintegrating right under her cute little button nose. "Because we do, you know," I added, waiting for her tear-filled eyes to turn to me as she realized we were all in this together.

And she did turn to me when I'd finished. But her eyes were dry. And instead of sharing a knowing look, she tipped her head to the side and said, "Huh?"

She had no idea what the hell I was talking about. "I meant," I stammered, but I had no idea what I meant anymore. What had started out as a Hallmark moment had turned into an awkward moment of silence.

The point: Yes, it's nice to let your friend's children know that you're there for them if they want to talk. But instead of turning sentimental because it feels like an *On Golden Pond* moment, perhaps it's better to simply say, "How're you doing?" and wait for your cue. If the answer is a cheery, "Dandy-O!" maybe it's not the time to offer a shoulder to cry on. If the answer is, "Fine," followed by the sniffles, maybe it's time to lend an ear.

No matter how good your intentions, kids don't want to feel like they're the main character in an Afterschool Special. So don't treat them like one.

Rule #2: Read Your Kids' Cues

Make the most out of what your children seem to be responding well to. Kids tend to focus on the strangest things. When a friend of Jennifer's and mine separated from her husband, and he moved out, instead of sobbing about the new arrangement, her son could not stop talking about the bunk beds he was going to have in his dad's new house. And her daughter couldn't wait to pick out her new room décor in the Pottery Barn Kids catalog. So while you're imagining your children with a permanent roller luggage attached to their left hands, with all of the back and forth, the fact is, your kids will probably get a kick out of choosing their "other" bedroom in their "other" house. This is not to say that a purple paisley quilt resolves all issues, but reading your children's cues can help you determine what they'll positively respond to in the coming months. In our friend's case, it was the novelty of having two rooms, two places the kids could call their own and feel in control even when the situation was decidedly out of their control. Does your son love basketball? Maybe that new hoop in Daddy's driveway, and the bonding experience of beating Dad at Horse every weekend, softens the blow of divorce just a little. Is your daughter a Kim Possible fan? Maybe her second home can have Kim's complete set of DVDs.

It's also quite likely—and yes, I am stereotyping—that Daddy's got better junk food at his place than you do at yours. Kids dig that, too. He probably also doesn't make a big deal if they want Fruit Roll-Ups and Tostitos for dinner (although you could probably run a close second with all the Happy Meals you pick up on your way home from work). Remind your children about the cool things associated with the new living arrangements. There may be more dinners out—what kid doesn't like eating out? There will probably be two birthday cakes and twice the number of summer vacations, and you can't go wrong with that. Focus on what's getting better, and don't forget to mention that they still have two parents who love them. That's one thing even divorce won't change.

The Divorced Girls' Society
TOOLKIT

It's Not Just a Happy Meal That Can Make a Kid Happy

There are a few simple ways to help make this transition easier for your kids. And if your kids' lives have less stress, Mommy's life has less stress, too. That's called a win-win scenario.

- Get some great picture frames and place photos of your child and Daddy, and your child and Mommy, at each house.
- Double up on a special item—stuffed animal, book, poster—so that no matter which house your kids are at, they feel at home.
- Stock both houses with life's everyday staples—toothbrush, PJs, underwear—so that your children don't need to lug supplies back and forth (and you won't get a call to bring over the sparkle cherry-flavored toothpaste).
- Let your children help decorate their new rooms and the rest of the new place as well. They'll feel more connected if they've played a part in how the place looks and feels.

Rule #3: Maintain the Status Quo
Logistics should be the only thing that changes—living arrangements, visitation, holidays. The problem is, it's very tempting to overcompensate for logistical changes by becoming afflicted with an ailment we've come to call The Mom Who Forgets She's in Charge. And the cause of this debilitating disorder? *Guilt.* It can take over every part of your body, consuming you like a bad case of eczema. When guilt starts to work its way into your thought process, it can distort even the simplest parenting responsibilities. It's so tempting to think, *The poor boy, of course he can have his head shaved in a relief of a monster truck—and that Satan's Son logo he'd like tattooed on his chest, that's fine, too! I mean, his parents are getting divorced!*

Guilt. It costs you, and not just because every time you go to Target you're going home with the latest Xbox game. No, it also undermines your role as the grownup. It erodes your ability to make your child feel secure, because all of a sudden *she's* the one running the show. And she can't even tie her shoes! So remind yourself that you should not be spending the equivalent of your monthly mortgage on a new sound system for Junior because you feel bad about his dad moving out. (For what it's worth, that sound system should be in your room, not his.)

Don't try to compensate for the end of your marriage by indulging your children. All of the things they hate to do? Continue to enforce those rules—hell, you may want to add a few more chores to the list. Those little cherubs—hah! It's as if they can sense that you're in a tenuous spot, and baby, they'll work you over so fast you won't see it coming. Don't let it happen. I am not saying children are nefarious little creatures at heart, but they can be opportunistic, and of course, everything they do is to test their limits. My four-year-old started claiming that she missed Daddy and wanted to sleep in my bed. The first few times I heard that my heart melted—my divorce was creating a four-year-old insomniac! I had overlooked the fact that she was always searching for a reason to join me in my queen-sized, 400-thread count covered space. But she was too smart: She homed right in on my Achilles heel—guilty parent going through a divorce. Foiled by a four-year-old! How could I not have seen it? Don't you fall into the same trap! Retain your hard candy shell, girl!

The way you are parenting should not change. In fact, I'd recommend wielding an even bigger parenting stick. Is your teenager giving you a hard time because she wants to make phone calls after 10:00 P.M., even though they are not allowed? Don't change the rules, even if there's one less person around to enforce them. Sure, she will probably hate your guts, start calling you by your first name, and unleash tirades about how evil you are. Soon thereafter, her clothes will start smelling like cigarettes, and her MySpace site will contain poems about self-mutilation. No, it won't come to that. On second thought, it might . . . if you start acting like a wimpy, weepy mom who spends more time focusing on her own marital problems rather than paying attention to the brooding fifteen-year-old living in her house.

The Divorced Girls' Society
GOLDEN RULES

So what's appropriate and what's downright unacceptable when it comes to dealing with your kids? Here's a sampling:

- Do be honest with your kids. I'm not advocating that you share every single morbid detail of yesterday's therapist appointment, but I am suggesting that kids feel more secure and at ease when they know what's going on. "Mommy and Daddy are working with someone who's going to help us figure out some complicated grownup stuff, and while we do that, Daddy won't be living with us anymore." Good. "Mommy's not crying; I am having an asthma attack—pass the inhaler." Not so good.

- Do keep up as much routine as possible. Soccer on Saturdays, church on Sundays. Yes, even leftover night on Monday, and the staying-up-late rule on Friday nights. Their lives should change as little as possible.

- Do realize this is a big deal for your children, and provide extra reassurances about how much you and their dad love them. So when your eight-year-old wakes you up in the middle of the night and asks what "divorce" means, and you fell asleep only an hour ago because you forgot to refill your sleeping-pill scrip, put on your happy face, have her snuggle next to you, and tell her. Make sure they know that they can come to you to talk about anything that is bothering them.

- Don't use honesty as an excuse to unload every feeling you're having onto your pint-sized housemate. "Mommy's sad because Daddy thinks it's okay to spend his 401(k) on a matching set of Ski-doos for him and his new girlfriend, Candy." Honest, sure. Too much information? You bet.
- Don't stress that your children might end up scarred for life because Mommy and Daddy don't live in the same house. The fact that your twelve-year-old daughter is hanging out with a multi-pierced, purple-haired dude named Damien is much more worthy of your concern.
- Don't stop parenting. You are first and foremost a mom, albeit a stressed out, Doritos-eating, nail-biting one. Reserve your self-centered behavior—which you are completely entitled to—for nights off without your children.

When the Hard Candy Shell Cracks

You try. You're a tough cookie. You hold it together. But every once in a while, you lose it in front of your offspring. Guess what? It's called being human. I knew I couldn't be crying all of the time in front of my little one, but there were times when I was feeling down in the dumps and I didn't try to paste a smiley face on. What children should know is that it's okay to be sad. And even though I did tend to reserve my crying fits for times when I'd have the least amount of onlookers—the drive to work, in bed at night, my therapist's office—as everyone knows, you can't plan where you sob. Sometimes it just overcomes you, and like the need to vomit, you just have to let it out, no matter how loud, ugly, or unappetizing the results may be. Will it damage your children for life if they see you crying? No! You're not an automaton (although you may have been accused of being one by your ex on more than one bad sex night). You, my dear, also have a soft, chewy center, and your children should know the hard, the soft, and that you are a great mom who cries when she needs to.

The Divorced Girls' Society
TOOLKIT

Cry, Baby, Cry

While the idea of blowing your nose through an entire box of tissues is bad enough, the thought of actually having your child witness your teary-eyed breakdown can be horrifying. You're supposed to be strong. You're supposed to make your kids feel secure. You're the *mom*, after all, and moms are unflappable, right? But even if moms sometimes exhibit superhuman abilities, we're not made of steel. And that's why you need to be prepared to explain to your kids why Mommy is sad or unusually quiet, or her eyes resemble those bloodshot eyeballs the costume store carries at Halloween time. So here are some ways to answer your child's questions about why Mommy seems down, or teary, or why she's eating Oreos for dinner the fifth night in a row. And may I make one more suggestion? Puffs Plus with Lotion— cuts down on the red, chapped nose.

- "Mommies can get sad, too, just like you do sometimes. But even when I'm feeling sad, I still love you a lot, and your smiles really help me feel better."

- "Crying is normal, and sometimes a person needs to cry just to get out their feelings. It doesn't mean I'm angry or upset with you."
- "It's better to let yourself feel the way you feel rather than keeping everything inside. Sometimes a person needs to cry, because it helps them feel better afterwards. And sometimes just expressing your feelings makes you less sad, even if it doesn't really change what's making you sad."
- "Mommy's quiet because she's thinking about a lot of grown-up things. It doesn't mean I don't want to be with you, I just need a little time and some silence right now."

Living la Vida Loca . . . in a 1950s Colonial with Two Kids and a Lab Named Rusty

Eventually you're going to have to address it. Your social life. Plus your kids. And the coexistence of both. Only with kids in the house, the equation isn't as simple as one plus one. It's more like one plus one divided by the number of children you have and multiplied by the number of years you've been out of the dating scene.

If your head isn't quite ready to wrap itself around the idea of sitting at a dinner table across from a man who's staring at your post-breastfeeding chest, you're probably thinking that this information is unnecessary, superfluous, and completely out of the realm of possibility. You wonder: *Why is she talking to me about this future state where I actually have a life? My life is my children and getting through this divorce. There is no need to see beyond that.* Wrong. You sweet, naïve, divorcing gal, there is life after divorce. And it can actually be more fun and more exhilarating than your married life! You will be asked out on dates, you will go out on Friday nights with the gals. So while you're currently not plotting how to sneak your lover out of the house in the early morning hours lest your children wake up and have their retinas singed by a man donning black silk boxer shorts, these things will come up at some point.

I keep one hard and fast rule: Let your children know that you have a social life. Mommy can't subsist on macaroni and cheese and Friday-night Disney Channel movies. They won't resent that Mom knows how to have fun with other grownups; in fact, it might be nice to see that Mommy isn't saving them a seat on the couch for another rerun of *The Parent Trap*. (*Hey*, you think, *at least it's the Lindsay Lohan version.*) But even if you do venture out into the dating world, it's probably best if your children don't actually meet your suitors. At least not until you're ready to make this new man a very significant part of your life—and theirs, too.

When I first started dating a guy regularly, I was somewhat elusive about who my "friend" was—not stating explicitly that it was a male friend, just a friend. My daughter eventually caught on that it was male, and probed a bit. I was candid, and said that I liked David and we have fun hanging out together ("Much like you like hanging out with your friend, Madeline," I'd say to her). That was enough to satisfy her curiosity. Then again, she's five. Remember, it's normal and natural to have a life outside of your children, a life with adult interaction (the romantic kind is included there), and it is something you should enthusiastically pursue in your new life.

Tips for Your SPEED-DIAL SISTERS

Friends can play a great role in helping your kids adjust to what's going on around them.

- Offer to take the kids to the park, out for ice cream, for a walk, anything that can give your divorcing friend—and her child—a break.
- A close friend can be another ear for your friend's kids; someone to talk to about what's going on and to voice things they might be afraid to say to Mom and Dad.
- If your friend's child says, "Don't tell Mommy," then don't. Now is a good time to teach a kid that they can trust adults, and that includes keeping promises. Also, it helps you build credibility for future conversations.
- That said, when a friend's child confesses feelings that are particularly worrisome, and you think it's in the best interest of all involved that his mom knows what he told you, then by all means tell. Your job is to be a good listener, but it's also to be a smart adult.
- Bring a favorite gift or special treat to your girl-friend's kids . . . just because. They're going through a big change themselves, and a little extra lovin' can mean a lot to them now.

What my daughter chose to tell my ex about my social life was irrelevant, as I well knew. Besides, he and I had already established a set of rules around when we would introduce important people in our life to our daughter, and agreed that we would share this information with each other before any child introductions took place. The last thing you want is to rely on your children to be the communicators of information as sensitive as meeting boyfriends and girlfriends of Mommy and Daddy. It's unfair to ask that of your children. Put a rule in place; for us, we agreed we would only introduce our daughter to people who were truly important in our lives—not just casual friends. (In other words, you'd never want your daughter to meet your FWB.) Because we had a system that was already in place, nothing else really mattered as it related to my dating life and my ex. Of course, when it comes to dating, there's a ton to consider, which is why Chapter 10 is devoted to the topic.

DIVORCED GIRLS' SOCIETY TENETS

- ✓ You may have stopped being married, but don't stop being a parent.

- ✓ Don't let the guilty mom in you influence your parenting decisions.

- ✓ Being sad around your kids is fine. Being in a perpetual state of tears is probably a sign of a problem.

✓ Having kids doesn't mean not having a social life. Know that it's perfectly okay to go out on dates, meet up with friends, or stay out dancing the night away. It's also okay to let your kids know that you are out having fun.

That's Not an "S" on Your Chest, or Why Playing Superwoman Might Not Be the Way to Go

Just like you probably tell your children when they ask about the oddly shaped mole on Aunt Effie's nose: People are different. A veritable smorgasbord of shapes and sizes; no two people are the same. This also applies to how we act when faced with life's dilemmas. We handle adversity in different ways. Some of us tackle the issues head-on, like a linebacker—black under-eye paint and all—while others of us prefer to tap out a delicate soft shoe, clicking solidly on top of some issues, delicately touching others (Fred Astaire top hat optional, kicky high-heeled tap shoes required).

When my divorce hit me like a giant cooler of ice-cold orange Gatorade, I took the linebacker approach, hunkered down, and charged ahead. It was as if the one big change wasn't enough. I wanted it all to change. Drastically. Monumentally. *Oh yeah? Think you can set my life into a tailspin with your cli-chéd middle-aged announcement? I scoff at your weak attempt at change: I'm selling the house, starting a new job in another state, changing my hair color, and getting a nipple pierc-ing. See how irrelevant your little change is to me now?* By wanting to make all of these other changes, it made the divorce change seem like no big deal at all.

The problem with that is—besides the fact that nip-ple piercing is just a bad idea independent of anything that's going on in your life—divorce *is* a big change. To be dealt with rationally and smartly, as I've been say-ing all along. It's not something that you should try to minimize by creating more drama in your life. You have plenty of drama now, thank you very much. And while it's unhealthy to become obsessively focused on it, it's also ill advised to add more adversity and upheaval to your life in order to pretend it's not there. You need to strike a balance.

Yes, use this big change as a catalyst to drive other big changes you want to make in your life. But don't do it all in one month. And make changes that you've thought through, that are important to you, that feel right. Don't change for the sake of change. If you can explain to your-self why you are making each modification to your cur-rent life, and it makes sense, that should be your litmus test. If, however, you try to rationalize your decision and it sounds like, well, rationalizing, then it's probably not a good idea to make that change. And, more importantly, do it because you want it for yourself—not to prove a point to other people, or to compensate for feeling out of control in other facets of your everyday existence. And for god's sake, don't do the nipple piercing.

The Divorced Girls' Society
TOOLKIT

The Good vs. the Bad Change

Whoever said change is good never went through a divorce. There are moments of sheer stupidity that can take over a once-rational, smart, and level-headed divorcing woman. Here are some things to watch out for:

Good Change	Bad Change
You've always wanted short hair, now's the time	Mohawk with "My Ex Sucks" etched into the side of your head
Switching to organic vegetables	Throwing tomatoes at your ex-husband's car as he drives by
You hate the minivan, so you sell it for a smaller, more economical sedan	You hate the minivan, so you sell it and buy a motorcycle
Drinking more water	. . . as a mixer with scotch

What, Me Worry?

You know this girl, maybe she's you: the one who shoots her hand up—smarty-pants style—when the teacher asks the questions. She's always first, always on the ball.

That's who I wanted to be in the eyes of those witnessing my divorce. I wanted to out-answer, out-prepare everyone else. So when concerned neighbors turned out their lower lip, feigning sadness at my situation, I would quickly offer up, "Oh, that? Yes, I'd almost forgotten, since there's so much else going on in my very, very full life." It wasn't about sharing the news, it was about making sure everyone knew I was four steps ahead of the news. And that my life was so filled with other things, this event was merely a blip on the radar screen.

MANTRAS to get you through the day

Ch-ch-ch-changes. . . .

Those were the kinds of emotions driving my need to change, change, change. I also wanted to declare to the world (and anyone who would listen) that I was an independent woman, and I didn't actually need my ex-husband. God, I had my shit together! "Miss Independence" was my mantra. And while my Kelly Clarkson impression didn't do much to garner praise or applause from my daughter, I had bought into the "do it all on your own" attitude, hook, line, and sinker.

Although I quickly discarded the idea of a tattoo spelling out KISS MY ASS across my shoulder blades, my first attempt at independence was just as extreme—I wanted a new house. I wanted to remove myself from the memories, and plant my independent stake in the ground (preferably in a restored row home in the downtown area). I wanted a complete and utter change in surroundings.

I wasted no time finding a realtor and setting aside two Saturdays that first month to go out to various parts of the city looking for what was going to be the setting for my new life. After all, I had to scrap the old and start with the new. I toured countless gutted Victorian row homes in not-yet-gentrified neighborhoods. "Get in now and you pay less," my realtor urged. He forgot to mention the homicide rate, or the fact that my new home's accent pieces would include bars on the windows.

We inspected dozens of homes in neighborhoods I had never even heard of before, and when I asked about the schools, my realtor deadpanned, "Private schools would be your best choice in this area." Later that afternoon I did an Internet search of crime rates. It was not reassuring. In fact, it was downright depressing.

But I wanted a change. I wanted everything to be new, different, and uniquely mine. I also wanted to make my own decisions, and I felt like the house I currently lived in was the result of a shared effort that no longer represented something I wanted to be a part of.

I didn't want the same house that, four years ago, I had walked through with my ex and decided—with him—that this would be the perfect home for our family. It certainly didn't seem perfect now. It was a reminder of our married life—from the wall of pictures that highlighted our annual vacations, to the antique snowshoes we bought at an auction in Vermont years ago. The whole house was a historical homage to our life together. I couldn't look anywhere without remembering a moment or an experience (potted ficus, circa 2003, picked up at Home Depot, or unfinished wine rack that stayed unfinished because we never could decide on a color of paint). I wanted nothing to do with it. I wanted a blank slate.

But the only blank slates that were in my price range required my owning a handgun for protection and a serious investment in private schools. Before long, the idea of moving to another house seemed less attainable, and less appealing. So I had another brainstorm.

The second big change I considered—however briefly—was leaving the state I'd come to call home. The world was my proverbial oyster, and Mama needed a new strand of pearls. I thought about Florida—my parents were there, and there were ample job opportunities for someone like me. The thought of being in the same city as my family—an idea that once sent a shiver up my spine—was appealing now, since I craved security and reliability from loved ones. I also toyed around with Massachusetts, since two SDSs lived outside of Boston.

I spent a few days checking out my job opportunities, and those Web sites where you type in what your salary is in your current city to see how much more (or less) you'd need to make in the new city. Working in financial services made the job opportunities pretty broad. That was reassuring. And then I looked at the cost of living. And wouldn't it just figure that the cost of living in my current city was pretty much lower than anywhere I typed in, except maybe the upper regions of North Dakota. It then occurred to me that no amount of love from a family member or best friend would make me more able to afford the kind of home I'd want to live in if I moved out of Virginia. Upon further consideration (funny thing about crazy ideas: if you give yourself enough time to think them through, the less appealing they become), I deep-sixed the idea. This was also about my daughter. And both her dad and I wanted her nearby. I owed him (and my daughter) that promise. And a brave new adventure in a mysterious new state was not worth my daughter only seeing her dad twice a year. I am, however, keeping the option of moving to a new state open when she turns eighteen. And it won't be North Dakota.

I was zero-for-2 of big changes implemented. Frustrated and disappointed, however I also knew I had made the right choice.

Idea!

Moving is tough, regardless of why you're pulling up stakes. If the circumstances of your divorce require that you move, there are some options that may make the idea, and the reality, more palatable. We have a friend who found a rental house just down the street from her old house. It was still in the same school district. The kids even got to stay on the same bus. Sure, the house was smaller than the one she once shared with her spouse, but it wasn't the size the kids were talking about when the moving truck pulled up. It was how great it would be to get on the bus five stops sooner and snag a better seat.

It doesn't take a genius to figure out that if there's one less adult living in the house, finances will get a bit tighter. So you're forced to take on a big change, but with some creativity you can find ways to make it work without turning your life upside down.

Sister, Can You Spare Some Change?

What did not occur to me was that the house I was currently in was not an unfortunate reminder of days past; it was the stuff *inside* the house. Namely, pictures on the wall and a few key items. Joint purchases that I wasn't necessarily 100 percent behind, but, because I was a team player, I compromised. I negotiated. I put my personal wants aside because there is no "I" in team.

What also did not occur to me was that there was a lot about where I was living that was actually still good. And still important to me. The house held memories of my daughter. She learned to walk up its stairs, she sat on the counter with me as a toddler and helped me make coffee in the morning. And there were the neighbors.

In a strange—sometimes troubling—way, you all are joined by some symbiotic neighborhood force. Your neighbors, they know you. They're the ones who see you in your boxers and T-shirt, glasses, and ponytail on Sunday mornings, teetering on bare feet in the driveway to grab the Sunday *Times.* The ones who, you hope, can't see from their vantage point that your breasts are doing a bit of a teeter themselves, since you are not wearing a bra. These neighbors are the same ones who saw your sunburned face and shoulders at the July Fourth picnic, have sampled some of your best and worst potluck dishes at the Labor Day block party. You all know what each other's house is worth, you can see whose house has the cleaning service showing up every other Thursday, and which houses have the screamy moms. There is a deep knowledge of one another that can only occur by living in close proximity each and every day. This can be a good thing, or a bad thing. In this case, I chalked it up to a good thing. A good thing because the whole neighborhood knew (and adored) my daughter. I felt like she was safe in our little cul-de-sac. For the first time, I took to heart that saying, and really believed in the "it takes a village" philosophy. No, we weren't living in thatched-roof huts and roasting goats on a communal campfire, but we were all connected, and that meant looking out for one another's children.

Big Changes, Little Changes

Obviously, there are super-sized changes going on in your life right now, and you shouldn't feel the need to minimize them or their impact. And I think I've effectively talked you out of making any life-altering decisions immediately after the big announcement that did, in fact, alter your life. But if you feel empowered to do something a bit crazy (again, not advocating the nipple piercing)—like a trip to Vegas with your best girlfriends (Speed-Dial Sisters are a logical choice here, but that Angelina Jolie friend of yours might also be fun here), or redoing a room in your house in your favorite color (lavender, anyone?)—then yes, have at it. Consider changes that are not life changing, but ones that change your frame of mind for the better. Buying a new home in a new area equals life changing. A weekend away with friends where you can misbehave a little (or a lot) does not equal life changing. Keep these in perspective and you should fare pretty well.

There are infinite changes you can make once you realize you're going to be going it alone. There are the big ones: selling the sweet colonial with the rooster wallpaper in the kitchen and moving into that loft downtown with exposed beams, neon wall art, and pendant lighting dangling from the ceiling. And the not-so-big ones: installing that alarm system you've always wanted but your husband insisted the baseball bat under the bed was all of the deterrent a wannabe thief would need.

I discovered a great way to determine the impact of the big changes, the middle-of-the-road changes, and the changes that were so minor as to seem to be no-brainers. For any change I wanted to make I simply thought: *What is the impact of this change today? In a week? In six months? In a year?* When you put things in those terms, it really allows you to see the impact.

Take moving houses, for example.

- Today I'd be thrilled. A new house! A place of my own. Can't wait to move in.
- In a week I'd be looking at all of the rooms of my house and thinking that, while packing everything up in boxes didn't thrill me, it wouldn't be that bad, right? Only, in addition to the inconvenience, there was the cost, and not just for the movers. There were closing costs and inspections. And any house I could afford would require some fixing up. There was no way I'd live with an acorn-encrusted dining-room chandelier flanked by the squirrel sconces.
- In six months I'd be in a new house, but the novelty would be wearing off. Maybe my daughter wouldn't have as many friends on our new street, and her school would be farther away. And, because the school didn't have an after-school program, I'd hope my neighbors would see her off of the bus three days a week. But I didn't even know who my new neighbors were, no less how willing they'd be to play Village.

- In a year I'd be in a new house, but you know what? I wouldn't be better off. I'd still be divorced. Only instead of finding comfort in the familiar, I'd be trying to figure out the unfamiliar. And that just didn't sound like as much fun as picking a new house to demonstrate my independence. It just sounded tedious. And like a big mistake.

Ego, Thy Name Is Me

While it was certainly tempting to want to demonstrate to the world that I was this grand, self-possessed woman who could do it all by herself, including living in my own home that I picked out by myself in the neighborhood of my own choosing, I was letting my ego get the best of me. And this was no small financial decision. In my eagerness to assert my newfound independence, I was shortsighted and didn't see that the house I was in now was the best choice. Close to work, close to all of my daughter's diversions, close to the neighbors that cared for us and our well-being. Sure, it was a planned community, and there were a hundred other families who lived in a house exactly like mine (the Chandler, model RK436, with the bonus morning room), but with all of the changes going on in my life, maybe now was the time to just sit tight and take it slow. And to focus on other changes that were taking place. So in my notebook, next to the word "House," I placed a check mark, to indicate all was in order. Nothing to change there. And I moved on to the next play in my playbook.

When setting out to prove things, either to yourself or to the world, you need to make sure you're doing it for the right reasons. And that the economics make sense. Sure, applying for that new job at work, the one that requires traveling the world in business class while getting wined and dined in fabulous restaurants, has more status. Of course your ego will be stroked every time someone asks what you do and the resulting title that flows out of your mouth stops them in their tracks because you are *oh-so-important*. But will that big new title on your business card make a difference when you're 4,700 miles away on your daughter's birthday? Or you're jetlagged on Thanksgiving and you've got fifty-three of your closest family and friends to cook for? While the added income would sure be nice at a time like this, what about the added child-care costs to cover all of those hours you're gone overnight, not to mention those nightly trips to Boston Market because Mommy didn't have time to make dinner?

The Divorced Girls' Society
TOOLKIT

Today's Change, Tomorrow's Mistake? Maybe, Maybe Not.

Have some changes you'd like to make? Before jumping in with two feet, or automatically discounting a change as a bad idea, try this. Write down the changes you'd like to make, and then figure out what the impact will be for different intervals of time (see the chart on the next page). It might help you gain some perspective before diving in, or show you that the change is a risk worth taking.

CHANGE	IMPACT			
	Today	One Week	Six Months	One Year

Remember that during this time, you don't need to prove anything to the world at large. Grand gestures of independence have ramifications that will be felt long after the tattoo scabs have healed. They make temporary tattoos for a reason.

DIVORCED GIRLS' SOCIETY TENETS

✓ Creating new drama doesn't make the old drama go away. It just adds more drama, and this play you're in now (called Divorce) is already a few acts too long.

✓ When you think about the change you want to make, consider the short- and long-term impacts. Getting a tattoo may feel and look right today, but when you're fifty? Not so much.

✓ Making something uniquely yours doesn't mean totally scrapping the old—it just means tweaking it to your liking.

✓ You may not be a superwoman, but you are super!

Looking for Love . . . or Just Someone Willing to Share a Buy-One-Get-One Pepperoni Pizza

Dating. It's not a concept I could even fathom in the first days of my marital decline. Okay, the first month. And the six months following that. You know what they say about getting back on the horse? Well, I'd never considered myself much of an equestrian. The whole idea seemed so daunting. Where was I supposed to meet a man? Work was off limits, as everyone in my office still thought I was going home to a doting husband (see Chapter 5, "Stage 1: Denial," page 77). If I sidled up to that cute guy in accounting and asked what he was doing for lunch, it might seem a little odd—especially since I never turned my expense reports in on time. My neighborhood? I lived in suburbia, not exactly teeming with hotties waiting to sweep me off my feet (more likely, settled married men waiting for me to sweep the leaves off my front walk).

And beyond the *wheres*, there was the *how*, and the *what*. How was I supposed to date? How was I supposed to find the time, when I could barely squeeze in a hair appointment to touch up roots that were beginning to give me the funky two-toned look of a 1980s punk band? Did I schedule dates between 4:00 P.M. conference calls with my product team and my daughter's 6:00 P.M. soccer practice? Then there were logistics to consider: He couldn't meet me at my house, but I didn't want to be out in public—what if someone saw us? What did I want? Was I looking for someone who'd been through what I had? Or did I want a marital virgin? The unanswered questions continued to pile up, and before long I had worked myself into such a non-dating lather, I was paralyzed, not to mention confused (although I did find time for the hair appointment, which meant at least I wasn't lathered up, confused, and striped to boot).

Dating Without Running Toward the Finish Line

There's something that happens when you've been married for longer than you ever dated—the idea that dating leads somewhere. Whether it led to going steady or exclusively dating or living together or marriage—the end result didn't matter; there was still an end result. And since I hadn't "gone steady" in decades, and the whole exclusively dating thing had led to cohabitation, which dovetailed nicely into marriage, I had a huge mental block. Mainly that I couldn't decouple the idea of dating from marriage. And the idea of marriage, well, that just seemed so unsavory. My internal dialogue went something like, If I meet a man that I like, we'll start dating, and then progress to sleeping together. Then come the regular weekends together. He meets my kid, he proposes, and faster than you can say "prenup," we're walking down the aisle.

I was moving at warp speed in my head, and in the process of overthinking this dating thing, I managed to overlook something very important: I hadn't even put myself in a position to go out on a date. I needed to get back out there and start meeting people. That was the goal. You can, and should, view dating and getting married as two separate, albeit related, activities. At least in the early parts of your dating life. Don't complicate dating; it's already pretty complicated as is.

MANTRAS to get you through the day

There's a great big wonderful world of men out there, and if I want, they're there for the picking.

Butterflies in Your Stomach at the Thought of Being a Social Butterfly

Interacting with people is a very basic human need. Humans are social creatures, though you may be feeling less than social these days. And your solitary hobbies, while nice, should not be the only things you embrace as single-status diversions. So even though you've become a master faux finisher, put down the wrinkled rag and take your computer off sleep mode. It's time to start meeting people—and I mean people of the opposite sex.

Think of dating as an opportunity to dust off those social skills, hone your conversational prowess, and extend your social network. Hate to use this cliché, but the one about kissing a lot of toads? It's because not everyone you meet is soul-mate material. In fact, the odds are that most aren't. I'm not saying your prince isn't out there, but that should not be your goal when you venture into the world of dating. Your goal should be to get your feet wet, relax, and have fun splashing around. Just make sure your floaties are securely on, and stay away from the warm pockets of water.

It's a Date!

Going out on a date should be thought of as an innocuous pastime to be enjoyed and, more importantly, not to be taken too seriously. Sure, it's easy to have panic attacks on the drive over, to check and recheck the application of your lipstick, to quickly call an SDS when the armpits of your silk T-shirt start showing sweat marks. And you haven't even begun the date yet! The good news: The guy is feeling exactly the same way.

The first time I went out with an online match (which was also the first time we met face to face), I was frantic and worried, though I did my best to hide that (the sweat marks notwithstanding). When I walked into the bar where we were to meet, after mentally high-fiving myself for not tripping over the mat in front of the door, I confidently walked over to him and introduced myself. I may have given the appearance of being all that and a bag of chips, but inside I was so nervous I thought I was going to throw up—and peeing my pants wasn't far behind. After about thirty seconds, I began to notice something that changed the entire dynamic of the evening: *This guy was as nervous as I was.* His hand shook as he lifted his glass to his mouth (it was either nerves or early onset of Parkinson's—come to think of it, he was pushing 50), and on more than one occasion he accidentally snorted after laughing. Once I realized we were both on the *Goodship Nervewracking* together, I relaxed, so did he, and we ended up having a few laughs that evening. Was there a click? Did my heart skip a beat when our fingertips accidentally grazed each other's reaching for our water glasses? Did the candlelight illuminate his blue eyes so intensely that I got lost in their dreamy azure-ness?

Snap out of it, girl, it's Internet dating, not a Nicholas Sparks book!

Hell, it may take twenty dates until you get lost in someone's eyes upon first gaze. That's not why you're out there dating. You're out there because it's loads of fun, once you get the hang of it. And even better, the anxiety level drops precipitously the more you get out there. While I can pretty accurately declare that there was no love match made that night, it was fun to get to know a guy, share a bit about myself (admit it, you do like talking about yourself—these dates you go on? You'll be doing lots of that.), and be a part of the social scene once again.

If You've Just Fallen Off the Turnip Truck (aka, You Didn't Know You Could Meet People on the Web)

If the Web is still foreign to you, or, more likely, if the idea of meeting people in cyberspace gives you the cyberwillies, that's okay. There are myriad other places where you can begin testing the dating waters.

- Most church organizations have singles networks, which will allow you to meet others of the same faith. Many of these groups don't even require that you attend their parish. Check those out by word of mouth, or just go to your local church and check out their bulletin board.

- Remember the "Piña Colada Song," the one where the woman and man place personal ads in the newspaper and end up finding love? Well, twenty-five years after that song immortalized looking for love in two-column inches, you can do that, too. Something to keep in mind, though: This medium doesn't allow you to "get to know" someone as fully as, say, meeting folks face to face in other environments. In other words, you may have a hard time figuring out, with 250 words or less, if he's the kind of person you want to meet. But, still an option.

- Ready for a real dating adventure? Take to the high seas on a singles cruise. Or maybe a singles resort designed to help the single mingle. Even if you don't find true love, you can still eat well and get a tan.

- Pressed for time? Don't want to waste a minute when you know just by the way a guy wears his hair slicked back with Vaseline that he's not the one for you? There are events for people like you. Speed Dating, Three-Minute Dating, and It's Just Lunch are a few organized ways to meet prospective dates without committing an entire night to the ordeal. They all have sites on the Internet with more information.

You Know You're Ready to Begin Dating When . . .

- You spot a cute cocktail dress on sale and instead of thinking, "My husband always said v-necks made me look as sexy as Dora the Explorer," you think, "That hot number with the v-neck will bring my first date to his knees. I'll take it!"
- Instead of nervously looking away when a handsome man smiles at you, you smile back (but don't wink, leave a little to the imagination).
- The thought of kissing another man doesn't give you the dry heaves, the cold sweats, and a rash that resembles a relief map of Africa.
- Instead of saying no to your sister's invitation to play tennis (because you are tired of her killer backhand and the silly chicken-like victory dance she does on the other side of the court), you say yes because you realize that you've always liked a guy in tennis whites. You actually recommend a weekly game, and start putting on a full face of makeup before you meet.

The Sixth Circle of Hell, Otherwise Known as Internet Dating

When I decided it was time to enter the deep end of the dating pool, I knew where to start. It seemed everyone and their brother was on Match.com. With laptop securely propped on my knees, cordless phone crooked under my ear, I called Jennifer and together we tackled my profile. Creating a profile that really and truly reflects who you are is not an easy task. It required some writing, rewriting, lots of editing, and a girlfriend with the proper perspective. It didn't hurt that the girlfriend I chose to help me with my profile was also a published novelist. This sounds like a no-brainer, but your profile should really represent a snapshot of you. It should not read like all of the other profiles, because, sweetie, you're not like all of the rest. Who you are needs to stand out, needs to break through the profile clutter.

Stand out, you say? *I'm a thirty-five-year-old mortgage broker with two kids, living in the suburbs of Philadelphia, how am I going to stand out?* You're going to stand out because your girlfriend will help you. She'll be the one to call out those qualities in you that you may not even recognize exist. Get together with her and map out your interests, no matter what they are. Then make them fun. For example, if you collect salt and pepper shakers, say something like, "An eclectic collector who enjoys scouring flea markets for fun finds." Have fun with it, that's the key. Always keep your eye on the dating-profile ball: You want to come across as someone that the right guy must meet—but you must always, *always* be yourself.

You are irresistible, smart, sassy, with a killer sense of humor. The thing is, you can't actually say, "I'm smart, sassy, and have a killer sense of humor." It's just not terribly convincing. It's like if you have to tell people you're funny, then guess what? No amount of clown makeup or whoopee cushions can compensate for the reality. That's why the old adage, "show don't tell" works perfectly here. Don't tell prospective dates you love sports, show them. This can mean demonstrating your expertise in a favorite sport ("club badminton champion three years running"), using language a sports-addicted companion would understand ("still remember the first time I shanked a three iron into the sixth fairway"), or even posting a picture of yourself shushing down a black diamond. Choose words and pictures that demonstrate your personality.

You, Only Better—and Not Exactly You, Either

The key here is to make sure it's *your* personality on display—and not someone you always wanted to be. Jennifer and I had a friend who let us read her profile, and she sounded like a female James Bond: adventurous, well-traveled, nerves of steel. The only thing missing was her Secret Service code name. The thing is, when we read her profile we didn't even recognize the person we knew. Adventurous? This was a woman who in college refused to drive over the Massachusetts border because she thought they spoke French in Vermont. Nerves of steel? We'd seen her get rattled when the counter guy mistakenly skipped her number in the deli line.

The point is, the Internet isn't about wish fulfillment. If you want to be James Bond, you better be able to back it up with the Aston Martin, or at least a killer British accent. Be honest, with prospective suitors *and* with yourself. Maybe your idea of a great Friday night is eating take-out Chinese while watching *Jeopardy!*. Don't try to sound oh-so-hip in your profile. Tell it like it is. That's the only way you'll end up with someone who shares your penchant for kung pau chicken and a night with Alex Trebek.

The Divorced Girls' Society
TOOLKIT

Some Internet Sites to Get You Started

Don't know where to begin? Try a *few*!

Match.com. This is like the NYC of dating—only you don't get a map. It's big, it's overwhelming, but there's something about that that is really, really fun. Like NYC, Match.com is exciting, energetic, upbeat. But know this: You are on your own—thrust out there with your profile and whatever pictures you decide to post. Anyone can "talk" to you, and you can "talk" to anyone. No filters, no safety check, just one big Internet-meeting orgy. It's conceivable that a guy could want to meet you just because he thinks you're hot and you live in the same town he does. That doesn't exactly sound like the setup for finding the yin to your yang. But again, keep it in perspective. Match.com is a fun first place to test the Internet-dating waters.

eHarmony.com. This is like the Jewish mother of dating. Thorough, specific, structured, matching personalities and intellect—all that's missing is the guilt you get if you say no to someone, and the matzo-ball soup.

Engage.com. Remember the Clairol commercial? You'll tell two friends, and so on? This is sort of like that. If you really want your friends involved (SDSs would be great for this), then sign up for this site. It's a way for people close to you to participate in helping you find your match.

Goodgenes.com. If you're all about meeting some well-educated suitors (and you've also attended a Seven Sisters or Ivy League school), then a site like this may be appealing to you.

Rightstuffdating.com. Similar to Goodgenes.com, to join you must be a graduate or faculty member of their group of "excellent schools." You *will* have to show proof of your excellent-school status, by the way.

Singleparentmatch.com. This site is specifically geared to single mothers and fathers.

Get the Girls Involved

My foray into the World Wide Web of dating took place on Match.com. I spent a night writing a profile that I thought captured my essence perfectly. I included my likes, how I enjoy spending my time, and a picture that represented a realistic portrait of the woman they might be dating. When I finished, I sat back and smiled, satisfied with the effort.

And then I showed Jennifer what I'd written. And she laughed at me. And not in a good way.

What I learned, in addition to the fact that Jennifer's laugh can be quite bloodcurdling, is that, when it comes to seeing ourselves through a crystal-clean lens, sometimes we're wearing rose-colored glasses. It wasn't that my self-portrait was inaccurate, it just wasn't all that compelling. Where was the sense of humor, the spirited snarkiness? Jennifer decided to take matters into her own hands and offer some well-needed writing assistance. So I ceded control and let her have a shot at it. And what I got back wasn't just a very appealing me, it was a profile so tantalizing and accurate, I wanted to date me! See for yourself.

Yes, what you are about to read really is the first profile I posted on Match.com. And, yes, looking at it now I can see Jennifer's point. Hopefully, you'll be able to see it too.

What you write: For me, a great evening is one where I'm in my kitchen and enjoying a good bottle of wine. I love all kinds of food and enjoy discovering new cookbooks with unusual recipes. I don't need to go out to have fun.

What he reads: I'm a loner. I don't like to go out. I may also have an eating disorder, and/or may be using food as a psychological crutch. I'd rather sit in my kitchen drinking myself silly while I flip through cookbooks filled with recipes I'll never actually make because they require ingredients like orange zest and unsweetened coconut milk. I'm drinking straight from the wine bottle and have a Merlot mustache. I'm a very lonely, sad woman.

And now, after a little girlfriend magic.

So much better: Nothing beats a night of good food, good wine, and good friends. Who needs a stuffy restaurant to have fun and eat well? I'd rather have my friends sitting around the kitchen island, laughing and sharing stories while I whip up my famous spaghetti carbonara. Don't get me wrong, I love a night out on the town, but sometimes there's nothing better than hanging out with the people who totally get your sense of humor.

See the difference? It's still you, only turned up to eleven. With a little help from your girlfriend, you've written your profile, and now the matching begins.

What Your GIRLFRIEND *Is Thinking*

God, Vicki's first profile was *so* bad. It was the polite, air-kiss-on-cheek version of Vicki. Toned down, well behaved, oh-so-mature. She drank fine wine, enjoyed fine food, and liked nothing more than a quiet evening in her kitchen perusing cookbooks. A man wouldn't want to date her, but he might want her to babysit his kids while he went out with a woman who had a little more, shall we say, *personality*.

It took a giant leap of faith for Vicki to relinquish her login name and password and let me get to work. I didn't set out to create a wild woman who'd attract hordes of men. I just wanted the real Vicki to shine through. The woman who laughs so hard the wine she's drinking shoots through her nose. The woman who enjoys tuna melts as much as filet mignon.

If you aren't willing to give your profile over to a friend, at the very least, use your friends as a sanity check. A fresh set of eyes that can provide input on your output. And if you're really brave, close your eyes and let your friend write about the woman she knows.

While it may be a little nerve-wracking, wondering if a friend will come back with a profile that talks about your absent-mindedness and poor sense of direction, give her a shot. She loves you, and most likely, the profile will reflect you at your most lovable.

How to Make Your Profile Stand Out and Show the True You

Your profile is generally made up of two parts: answering some questions that ask for superlatives in the response (favorite, best, most enjoyable, worst—you get the idea), and then photos. To make the most of your profile, follow these tips:

The photo: Action and candid shots are always more believable. One guy I was matched with had one of those corporate, annual report-like pictures in his profile. To be sure, he was cute, but how uninteresting, and what was I supposed to take away from that picture? That he wore a suit to work? That he defined himself by his job? I also looked at a few men who included pictures with their children. As a mother, I thought that it sent the clear signal that this was a devoted dad, a family guy. But when it comes to including photos of kids, maybe think twice. Do you really want a picture of your child out there in cyberspace? Including family pictures is a personal judgment call. Things like pets, activities, and places you enjoy all make for great pictures though. And it goes without saying, smile!

The profile: Don't state the obvious. "I'm looking for an honest person." Well, yeah, it's not like any of us are out there in search of a pathological liar. Demonstrate your passions, be upbeat and positive. If you need to round out your profile, consider including descriptions of a perfect night, a perfect day, your favorite vacation, what makes you laugh, what makes you smile, and your ideal date.

The screen name (yours and his): Would you want to date *horneydude69*? Spend an evening with *2shortn-stubby*? Screen names speak volumes, because you choose them. Can't do much about mom naming you Morticia because she was a huge *Addams Family* fan, but here's your chance to create your own identity. *Lonely gal4u* might not be your best option. *Bustychick36dd*? Not unless you're seeking *hunglikeahorse*. How about choosing a screen name that really tells something about you, like *loves2ski*? Whatever you choose, don't get too hokey. First impressions are everything here, and your screen name *is* that first impression.

Deciding Who to Pursue or, Where's My Diamond in the Rough?

You're a modest gal, so you may not believe this, but once you go on these Internet dating sites, you will get bombarded with responses. Your dance card will fill up faster than you can say, "DWF seeks DWM for sunset strolls and good times." Your suitors will be lining up like the 737s at O'Hare. Now comes the fun part: choosing who you want to go to the next step with. And there's no fear of "how do I break it to him," because these Internet dating sites have all of these easy one-click buttons that make the bad and the ugly disappear.

When you're at the site, think of sorting through the dating profiles like you sort through the mail: must read, put aside to read later, and junk. Much like you can blow through your postal pile in a matter of seconds, this exercise in the Internet-dating space is similarly quick and painless. It goes something like this:

Pile A (must read): This guy clearly isn't Matthew McConaughey's twin, but he's still easy enough on the eyes. His profile includes phrases like, "When I'm not piloting my own plane, I am volunteering at the local pet

shelter . . . " and " . . . my ninety-three-year-old grandmother who I visit each Sunday. . . ." He seems to have
the perfect balance of confidence and humility. Time to
click to the next level.

Pile B (put aside for later): His profile makes him lik-
able, and his picture is appealing to you as well. But he
also discloses the fact that he has three dogs, a potbellied
pig, four children—and is the primary custodial parent
to all. Wow, that's a lot. You shudder at the thought of
four anklebiters and how frantic this potential suitor's
life must be. Quite honestly, you don't know that you're
up for this just yet. And while the rest of him seems
delicious, that one detail is a turnoff. Put him aside and
give yourself time to consider if the pros outweigh the
cons.

Pile C (junk): What a hottie. He *is* Matthew McConaughey's doppelganger. But, wait, that actually *is* a picture of Matthew, and you recognize it from last week's
issue of *People*. This creepy guy actually used a fake picture of himself—choosing the shirtless one to boot? And
chose a well-known celebrity? Where's that "No thanks"
button? You can't click it fast enough.

Once you've sorted each respondent into their bucket,
now it's time to spend a bit more time with the potential
keepers. Read the profiles, make mental notes—better
yet, take *real* notes. While creating an Excel spreadsheet
may be overkill, a nice little spiral notebook will help
you keep track of the influx of interesting suitors. Write
down the parts of the profile that resonate with you.
Maybe he's read some of the same books you consider
faves, maybe he likes that same hole-in-the-wall restaurant that you didn't think anyone else knew about.
Those similar interests are the things that will give you

stuff to talk about. Write them down so you don't forget. This way you won't be chatting away about Shakespeare with the guy who considers the back of a Bud can heady reading.

Share with Your Friends, Just Don't Hit "Reply All"

Whether or not you choose to share the correspondences with your girlfriends is your choice. It can be helpful—as in, your friend can probably provide a reaffirming thumbs-up when trying to decide whether or not a guy is worth responding to. She can also help you spot characteristics that you may not have noticed. I not only provided Jennifer with 24/7 access to all of my Internet dating sites, we also spent hours on the phone together laughing uncontrollably at messages from men like *Tan-and-Trim,* who responded with gusto that they were dying to meet me.

One important warning, however, if you choose to include your friend in the process: Make sure your cybersuitors don't know it. I had the unfortunate experience of forwarding an e-mail from a potential interest to Jennifer with a quick, "Think this guy's a goober?" Little did I know that I hit reply instead of forward: an easy enough, though devastatingly embarrassing, mistake to make. So now a guy I actually thought was kind of interesting knew that I thought he resembled a chocolate-covered peanut.

In the throes of the Internet-dating review—which can get pretty exciting and intensive—just remember to slow down and think about what you're doing before you do it. Said "goober" revealed to me that he saw the message, and quickly ended all future communications.

Another warning about Internet dating: If you're not in a large metropolitan area, prepare for the fact that you may actually know the person you're e-mailing before you meet him. Or at least, someone you know may know the someone you are e-mailing. A similarly embarrassing moment occurred when I realized that cyberdude worked at the same company my neighbor did. I e-mailed her asking about him, and she inadvertently forwarded the message to him, not realizing I didn't want to be revealed (damn that forward/reply mixup!). A series of made-up stories about my wanting to pursue a job opportunity entailed, and he was none the wiser. Nevertheless, the gaffe made me realize that even a medium-sized city can feel like a small town when you're talking about the singles world. (There was one positive outcome of that fiasco: Turns out the guy in question was a greasy, smelly smoker with a misogynistic point of view, and my friend strongly advised me to stay far, far away.)

The Divorced Girls' Society
GOLDEN RULES

Internet dating is a world ripe for some Golden Rules.

- **Do assume positive intent.** There are many out there like you—recently finding themselves without a partner, wanting to meet new people. Some of these men might not be the most eloquent of writers. Maybe they insert so many LOLs that the last thing you're doing is laughing out loud when you read their messages.

Know that some people communicate better in the written space than others. Cut them some slack and try to see beyond the smiley-faced emoticons. :-)

- **Do be discerning.** Your time is precious. Don't respond to, or agree to meet, every male who expresses interest. This may seem in conflict with the previous "do," but it isn't, because you will (hopefully) go through a dozen or so e-mail/phone interactions before you actually meet. If, after assuming positive intent and spending enough e-mail time to get a good idea of what a guy's all about, you feel like it's not happening, go ahead and end the interaction.

- **Do keep things in perspective.** You are not searching for your soul mate. You are searching for a nice, polite, socially well-adjusted human being to go out for moo shoo pork, and laugh over the way the instructions on the Chinese chopsticks read, "Have fun and eating too with authentic Chinese meal." This is about enjoying your free time (and some pork-stuffed pancakes) with members of the opposite sex, nothing more.

- **Don't force the issue.** If you are resisting any and all messages from your "matches"—or finding fault in every little detail of every guy that wants to meet you—chances are, you're not ready for this. Don't force the interaction. Let your membership expire until you are ready.

- **Don't be a bitch.** So your match turned out to be a mismatch. That doesn't mean you can begin pointing out all of the reasons he's wrong for you—or why he's an affront to all womankind, for that matter. Or ask why his profile said he was six-foot-six when he has to ask the maître d' for a phone book to sit on. Be kind. Be considerate. If you don't like a guy, then don't pursue next steps. But remember, he's in the same boat you are: Do unto others as you'd like them to do unto you.

- **Don't provide too much information.** This becomes an easy mistake to make, because the Internet has a funny way of making you feel comfortable around someone you've never met. But just because the veil of cyberspace makes you feel anonymous, don't start sharing the most intimate details of your life with someone you've never even met face to face.

The Internet-Dating Journey—Hold On to Your Parachute

If you start e-mailing a prospective date, and you and he appear to be getting along, resist the urge to begin disclosing personal information. Because as great as you think he might be, you still haven't met him, and so much can change. You're a modern girl, you know there is a creepiness element to the Internet. Internet dating has its share of oog-you-out kinds of guys. Keep that filter on when sending the backs and forths. You do not want to give him any more information than he actually needs. Save identifying details—your address, the name of the company where you're employed, ATM passwords—for later. Much later. At this point, the man at the other end of the information superhighway doesn't need to know your bra size to ask you on a date.

Remember, we all sound great in e-mail. E-mail allows us to craft the optimal response, to spin a web of magic and intrigue in which to attract the opposite sex. But it's not reality, and it's no replacement for actually meeting someone. Which means, at some point, the e-mails should progress to an actual face to face.

The Face-to-Face Meeting

You've done a few backs and forths, you feel comfortable, you've traded the barbs, and you actually like this guy. So when he asks to meet with you, assuming you feel good about this and want to, then accept the meeting. What you don't want to happen is for the e-mailing to evolve to a more intimate level before you've actually met the guy. In other words, if you're having cybersex with him, but haven't actually met him, back away from the laptop.

In planning the face to face, pick a spot that is convenient, crowded enough so you don't feel like the only people in there, and preferably with no alcohol on the menu. As tempting as it may seem to meet at a bar and allow that liquid courage to enable a more enjoyable time, don't do it. Stick to coffeehouses. Pick a date and time, and a few days before, call to confirm. Also helpful, is to tell your new male friend what color shirt you'll be wearing, so he can spot you easily. It reduces the stress significantly. Besides, those postage-stamp sized pictures aren't that sharp, so he may have you pegged as a Winona Ryder look-alike, when in fact you're more likely to be mistaken for Wynonna Judd. Make it so you can find each other quickly, and get to the business of getting to know each other.

Good and Bad Spots to Meet—and Things to Consider
Good Spots
- **Coffee bars.** The "salons" of our generation. Go there, find a cozy spot near the fireplace, or two overstuffed leather chairs in the corner, and have yourselves a relaxing afternoon.
- **Sandwich/bread franchises.** These places are everywhere. For a culture that is so carbophobic, it seems almost sacrilegious to frequent these. But they generally serve coffee (and myriad breadlike products—braided challah anyone?), and they are quiet and neutral.
- **City parks/museums/public recreation areas.** Good choice if you are an outdoorsy gal and you've made a date with same. You have the chance to go on a nice walk, enjoy the surroundings, and if the conversation lags, there's always the "Hey, isn't that a rare spotted yellow-bellied sap sucker?" to get the conversation going again.

Bad spots
- **Bars.** Alcohol can bring out the best—and worst—in people. Since there's no telling how it will affect the parties, best to avoid it. Bring it on, however, if a second date is mentioned.
- **Movie theaters.** How on earth will you be able to peer into his baby-blues when he's sitting to your left? And unless you can read lips, you'll get shushed faster than you can say pass the popcorn.
- **Places with too many children.** Because the noise level can be distracting, best to avoid places like science museums, playgrounds, elementary-school

lunchrooms (not that you would ever recommend an elementary-school lunchroom, but you never know, he might).

- **Libraries.** The lip-reader thing would come in handy here, too.
- **Places that are reminders of your past life.** I'm not talking reincarnation here, I'm talking about your married life. Don't pick Harry's Wing Emporium and Beer Hall if that's where you and your ex watched college football every Saturday afternoon for five straight years. There are plenty of other great places to meet your guy. Don't pick a place that means something to you from your married life.

Things to Consider
- **The length of the date.** Shorter is better for several reasons. Remember that expression, "Always leave them wanting more"? If things are going well, that old adage applies. Ever hear the expression, "I couldn't get out of there fast enough"? Think of a six-course meal at a French restaurant with a man who spends the first three courses talking about his foray into chest-hair waxing. Make it short and sweet. You can always see him again if you want to. And if you don't want to, you'll be thankful you heeded this advice.
- **Who will pay?** Your credit card or mine? Sound crass? Think again. I always assumed that whoever asked for the date would be the one to pay for the date—until my friend pointed out that she didn't see it that way. Maybe allowing the man to pay

creates a sort of inequality from the get-go. Maybe paying for yourself helps you feel less like this is a date, and more like two people getting to know each other, which will ease the tension a little. Whichever payment plan you decide to go with, knowing up front how you'd like the tab to be handled makes it a lot less awkward when the check arrives.

- **The date's end.** I know it might seem premature when you don't even know what he looks like without an eHarmony logo above his head, but even before a date begins you should think about how it will end. You meet for coffee and are having such a great time, you'd like to extend the date to dinner. Or you meet for coffee and are ready to call it quits before the steamed milk is hitting the bottom of your Starbucks cup. In either case, it's helpful to determine ahead of time how the date will end, and when. If there's obviously a connection, stretching the date seems like a great option. But there's something to be said for stepping away and, instead, planning a second date. You don't want to use up all your best stories the first time out, right? Likewise, if it's been downhill since you said hello, knowing that you had a thirty-minute commitment will make you feel that you've given him a chance. After all, he did drive to meet you, the least you can do is let the guy finish his mocha latte.

You Were Expecting Your Soul Mate, and Now a Lesbian Lifestyle Is Something You'd Consider

Make sure you set appropriate expectations when you meet your Internet amigo. Sure, he may have looked great in the pictures, but what if they were ten years old? And yeah, he seemed to have your similar sense of humor, but what if it only manifests itself when writing under the screen name *LoveMonkey*, and in person he's shy? Maybe he has gone on and on about how well-read he is, and you imagine meeting an extremely erudite guy who lets five-syllable words roll off his tongue with ease. Maybe another guy talks up how people always mistake him for Tom Hanks. You'll go to each new meeting anticipating something different and new. Will it be nerve-wracking and will you want to cancel each rendezvous thirty minutes before it actually happens? Yes, you will. But SDSs can talk you out of your low moments, so get them on the phone as you make your way toward Joe's House of Java, and get them to remind you why you're doing this, and that you're fabulous, and if it doesn't work out, won't it be a funny story?

Go into this assuming positive intent, keep an open mind, and have fun. If nothing else, you have increased your sphere of contacts, you have practiced how to be an engaging and witty conversationalist, and you got a free latte.

Step Away from the Computer

Remember that old-fashioned concept of being introduced to someone without having to enter a password and click a mouse? Well, it still exists. Sometimes, the best opportunities to meet new people come from old people—friends, coworkers, family. If someone claims to know the perfect guy for you, you might want to give them the benefit of the doubt. The fact is, while setups and blind dates may seem like a throwback to the days of yore, chances are someone who knows you will have a pretty good idea of what you're looking for. If you believe that, then using your networking skills to put the word out that you're looking for someone to share a Danish and cappuccino with on Sunday afternoons is a great idea. Just remember that leveraging your network of friends and family is one thing—requiring a weekly status report detailing their progress in setting you up with eligible men is another.

While the personal nature of networking is a plus, there are some things to keep in mind. If the person you're being set up with is also a boss's brother, a friend's coworker, or a relative's neighbor, you can't simply hit the delete button and wash that man right out of your hair. Instead, you'll have to explain why you didn't click, revisiting every detail of your afternoon at the aquarium. You may even have to defend your decision to excuse yourself before he could explain, yet again, why he believes he was a dolphin in a former life.

DIVORCED GIRLS' SOCIETY TENETS

✓ Get out there and date. The only commitment you are making is to yourself, to become social again.

✓ Spend a little extra time developing a great profile, something that truly reflects who you are, and doesn't make you seem like all of the others.

✓ Have fun with this new part of your social life. Enjoy reading through other profiles, see who you're interested in, who's interested in you, and go out on dates.

✓ You're not out there to find the next guy to walk down the aisle with—you're just looking to enter the social scene again—to try out those new restaurants and dance clubs with some eye candy at your side. Keep your new dating objectives in perspective.

Divorce Milestones, or Aren't We There Yet?

Space Mountain at Disney World always bothered me. Not so much the roller coaster itself—it's actually pretty tame as far as roller coasters go. It was the not seeing anything while plunging to my death in the dark that made me more than a little uneasy. For the entire ride, I had no idea whether I was going to plummet 200 feet or whip around a corner, and since I was in complete darkness there was no way to prepare for what came next. While a ride that lasts mere minutes might not be the best analogy for a process that can last years, Space Mountain has a lot in common with divorce. It forces you to acknowledge and deal with the unknown.

While I was going through my divorce, the planner in me wanted to know what was around the corner, what to expect, so I'd know when to relax and breathe a sigh of relief for a few minutes, and when to hang on tight and prepare to scream.

Just as there are five emotional stages you will need to work through, there are also five big milestones that you will have to navigate through. Thankfully, these are milestones that you can see coming and prepare for—even if that preparation won't make them any more palatable. Unlike the five stages of grief, the five divorce milestones are concrete, tangible, with a start date, and for most, an end date. An end! Yes, you can actually mark these off on your calendar. They are not nebulous psychological states of being, they are actual moments that you can check off your to-do list (in that cute little book you've been keeping for notes) as you go through them.

MANTRAS to get you through the day

Five giant steps for my divorce, one huge step toward my new life.

So, you're feeling a bit better about these five milestones, right? Well, not so fast. See, the tricky thing here is, there's no telling what kind of emotions these five events will bring on. They could conjure up world-class sobbing and uncontrollable body twitches. Or, they could be the reason you finally break out that fancy bottle of champagne you've been storing in your refrigerator's vegetable bin since 2004. There's no way to know how you'll react until they happen. They're kind of like giving birth in that way. You know the process, you have a due date, but you don't really know what you will experience until that day in the hospital when you're spread-eagle in all of your feminine glory, pushing your insides out.

Milestone No. 1: When He Moves Out/ You Move Out

Whether you're the one packing your bags, or the one staying behind to finally utilize all of the empty space in that king-sized closet, this is a big deal.

- You're the one staying in the house you both used to call home: For the person who stays in the old house while building a new life, there's no other way to put it—this feels strange. If you've been counting down the days until he walks out the door, you might also feel a sense of relief. Finally!
- You're the one leaving: When you leave behind the house you once shared, you're also leaving behind a lot of memories. Remember when you planted that sapling in the front yard? Now it's shading the driveway on hot summer days. That spot in the living room, the one where the sun streams through the window and creates a perfect napping spot on cold winter afternoons? You'll miss that. Leaving your home can be sad, but it can also be liberating. A fresh start. And while the new place will take some getting used to, you will get used to it. And you'll find the sunny spot in the new living room sooner than you think.

Flying Solo at Home

On the one hand—whoopee! The house is yours and yours alone! You can now parade around naked as a jaybird and not worry about alarming (or worse, turning on) your estranged husband, because he's no longer there! On the other hand—you're now the only adult in the house, a house that can feel so much bigger (a good thing, who can't use more space?), but also emptier . . . perhaps even scarier? Who will lock up every night, and then run downstairs at 3:00 a.m. to check on that strange noise coming from the dining room? Fuse boxes, heat pumps, and septic tanks? Taking the garbage to the curb every Tuesday morning? Yes, that now falls under your jurisdiction. There are good and bad things here at a very practical level. You can make the house exactly what you wanted it to be. Ex-husband not a fan of French-country décor? Always hated that sleek metal chair that he insisted was avant-garde and you always thought was just plain ugly, not to mention uncomfortable? Out with the chair, in with the floral drapes. You can always ask a friend to help you navigate the pink-foam insulation in the attic while you find that pesky leak in the roof. And the Yellow Pages exist for a reason. When the toilet overflows, look under "P" for "plumber." There are plenty waiting for your phone call.

If it seems like the house is a bit empty once you're alone, you may want to move some furniture around to better accommodate the living spaces. You may also want to do a quick inventory of the reminders hanging on the walls and resting on display (maybe you've already done this, and if you have, you go girl!). Remove pictures that no longer represent how you see your life, or remind you of things you'd rather put in the past. Arrange things to your liking. Always hated that clock over the refrigerator? Take it down! That garage sale find—the portrait of a hausfrau standing over a kitchen hearth—the one that your ex hated? Dig it out of the attic and hang that baby up! This is your house now.

Turning Your Newly Single House into a Home

First, make a list of everything your former spouse did around the house. The good news is, you'll probably be pleasantly surprised at how little he contributed. The bad news is, if your list ends up containing items like mowing the lawn, this will still need to be taken care of. Your grass doesn't stop growing just because the mower man has moved out. On the other hand, if it was something like whipping up vegan dinners, you can probably work around that—you never much cared for soy-based lamb-flavored chops anyway.

Use this list to determine how those chores will be done from now on. While some tasks may fall to you, there are always other options. Your children, for one—assuming they are old enough to take on chores and may perk up at the idea of making some quick bucks for doing a small bit of labor. Teenagers in the neighborhood who may want to make a few extra dollars for shoveling your driveway. Of course there are always competent professionals. Making the list will allow you to pinpoint the things you must tackle first to ensure your household is a smooth-running machine. It will also help make the transition more manageable, as it's really not necessary to determine who will plow your driveway if it's only July.

Don't forget to ask your ex about the household matters that he will be transitioning to you; the more you know, the easier the changeover will be. But even if you forget to ask about the purpose of that lone pipe smack-dab in the center of your backyard, there might be others who know why covering said pipe with a row of hydrangea bushes might not be such a great idea. And those people are called neighbors. The people next door can be a great resource when it comes to household issues. Chances are, all of the houses in the neighborhood have some commonalities, and this can come in handy when it's the middle of January and you can't figure out how to read the oil-tank meter. I asked a friendly neighbor where the valve was to flush out the underground sprinkler system. It didn't hurt that I wore my Daisy Dukes that day and acted about as clueless as an ornamental lawn jockey. Okay, maybe not. But it is easy to leverage the male knowledge available from a few helpful guys in the cul-de-sac.

Don't start making big-time home improvements. You may feel somewhat entitled to customize your home—now that there's no one standing between you and that wall you've always wanted to rip out to make a bigger, better master suite. But don't forget, just because your husband has moved out, that doesn't mean he's not still half owner of the lovely little place you call home. If his name is on the mortgage, then household decisions should still take his input into consideration. You don't want him throwing a fit and using your remodel as leverage during divorce proceedings. Feeling like you need to change something in the house? Then go for the pine-scented candle instead of the vanilla, paint the bathroom, replace the runner in the hallway. Keep it simple and save the big changes for later. There will be plenty of time for that super-sized hot tub on the deck.

Don't neglect your home. Yes, it will be a bit harder to be the sole person responsible for all household maintenance, but the fact is, the homeowners association doesn't care that you haven't found anyone to mow your lawn since your ex moved out; but they do care that you've got amber waves of grain—four feet high—taking over your lawn. This isn't really about what other people think, or your neighbors' expectations. It's about ensuring that the environment you surround yourself with is comfortable. It's about maintaining the same standard of living you had before. It's about realizing you deserve to live in a house that's welcoming and homey and *yours*. It's understandable that you don't want to think about winterizing the deck furniture, or at least getting it into the garage, but you need to. Because, come spring, you'll want to be out on your deck enjoying the sunshine and a good book—not rigging up the mildewed lawn chair so it doesn't collapse every time you lean back to reach for your lemonade.

Learning to Live Alone—and Loving It

When my ex moved out, I hated walking past what used to be his walk-in closet. I'd pass by that empty space on the left side of our master bedroom and I could practically hear the echo of my footsteps. But instead of thinking about that space as empty, I started to think of it as space that needed to be filled. By me. What woman doesn't need a little extra square footage? But, in reality, the whole house was mine, and I didn't need to commandeer this one closet. I also decided that maybe my daughter should benefit from this newfound space, so we didn't fill the closet with my clothes and shoes.

Instead, we turned it into her dress-up room. She loves it. And now I don't have to walk by a big, empty closet each morning when I go to the bathroom. But don't worry, I've taken over the guest-room closet.

What Your GIRLFRIEND *Is Thinking*

Every day it's something, and that something sure makes my own life seem incredibly mundane. No *Law & Order* court scenes for me. No late nights e-mailing a prospective date who owns his own villa in Tuscany and parasails on weekends (when not volunteering for Habitat for Humanity, that is). And shopping sprees for a new outfit that screams, "I have my shit together and this judge is going to know it"? No reason for me to go in search of the perfect shift dress and proper pumps, no less an opportunity to parade it in front of the judge and his trusty bailiff, Rusty. God, my life is boring.

Milestone No. 2: The First Time You and Your Attorney Meet with Your Ex and His Attorney

You will meet with your attorney several times before this key milestone, and all of those meetings are leading up to this one. The big kahuna. The mama of all meetings—you and your soon-to-be-ex sitting across the table from one another, squaring off. It's so *L.A. Law,* so *Hollywood Wives.* This meeting—the second milestone of your divorce journey—kicks off the tone for the future interactions between you and your ex. In a perfect world (the one with unicorns and fairies—you know that one, right?), you'd never have to worry about meetings with your ex, no less your ex and two attorneys. The very idea that you would need representation for something as harmless as a discussion about stuff seems farfetched. After all, you used to share everything with this person—a bathroom, a refrigerator, a future. How it's all come down to who gets what can seem terribly distasteful. All this talk about money and assets seems more than a little gross.

The sad fact is that that's exactly what your relationship is reduced to at this point. Yours and his. His and hers. And viewing it this way may not be pretty, but it is practical.

You're both adults, you both want to keep more money in your own pockets, and less in the pockets of Dewey, Cheatham, and Howe. Unfortunately, both parties need to be pretty close to agreement in order to bypass the lawyer involvement. So, assuming you can't shake hands and part with an air kiss to each cheek, you will need to schedule a meeting at one or the other's lawyer's office. And you will talk about what you agree upon, and what the other wants. If you can stomach it, you may want to recommend (to your ex) that the two of you come to some early agreements about custody and assets; this will go a long way (and save you significant dollars, as the presence of an attorney means that time really is money).

Start with the possibility that this is the first time you've seen your soon-to-be-ex in a while. Add the fact that you're meeting in an attorney's office, and top it off with this occasion is costing you both some serious spare change to discuss serious stuff, and you see why this is a milestone. And an awkward one at that.

For me, this meeting was uncomfortable, and not just because I was still eyeball-deep in stage three of my grief: full-blown depression so intense that opening the refrigerator sent me into a quivering tailspin because the expired sour cream reminded me of our favorite taco place in San Antonio.

Our meeting was right out of a Lifetime movie—only my attorney didn't look like David Birney, and I was no Valerie Bertinelli (though I did resemble her somewhat in my junior high school days). There were big conference rooms, plush leather chairs, and bookshelves containing leather-bound tomes with gold-foiled titles. I felt out of place, nervous, and my blotchy, tear-stained cheeks (fresh from the short drive to the lawyer's office) weren't helping my case much, either. But here's what I learned: Don't let the environment get the best of you. It's just an office. Attorneys use the Xerox machine like everyone else (okay, they don't, they have paralegals who do that). The point is, don't let the surroundings intimidate you. You have your lawyer protecting you from all of the legal mumbo jumbo, so relax, be yourself, and let your lawyer do all of the stressing out. You're not paying her to be eye candy. This is where a trustworthy, confident attorney starts to be worth her weight in gold (though you may have felt you've already paid your weight in gold to her firm, with all of the bills she sends you).

You're On Your Way
This milestone shows you are getting closer to the division of assets, which, at least according to the law,

means you are getting closer to officially severing those marital ties. As you and your attorney work toward the best arrangement for you going forward, this might be a good time for you, also, to take internal stock of what's important to you and what you'll need to live the life you want long after the attorney bills stop coming. Remember the homework and note keeping I recommended earlier? That can go a long way at meetings like this. You need to know what your living expenses are, and know what you want from this separation. You need to be your own best advocate, and push hard for what you want.

Milestone No. 3: Your First Time in Court

Whether your divorce is an amicable parting of the ways or a knock-down, drag-out fight, there's a chance you will end up in front of the judge at least once. This step in the process happens when the negotiations taking place between you and your ex have come to an impasse. Neither one of you is willing to make a compromise, and as a result, you can't reach a decision. The judge steps in to hear the argument and make a decision based on the information. Which can be good or bad. Take, for example, the division of a large asset: a house. You say it's worthless, he says it's worth a mint. When it goes to court, the judge will ask for an impartial real-estate assessment, and then make a decision. Remember that Lifetime movie? Yup, this would be the court scene. There's a witness stand, a surly old judge, a court stenographer; yes, there's even a gavel. And here you thought they were props that simply added to the TV drama.

You sit at one table, your ex at the other. There's even an armed officer standing next to the judge. You will take the witness stand and it will seem rather cool, if you weren't so overcome with anxiety and nausea. This probably wasn't what you had in mind when you always thought about your moment in the spotlight. But, for this milestone, you are the center of attention, and your time in court is your opportunity to show the judge who you are. The stay-at-home mom who's kept her family on keel, the working mom who still manages to make peanut butter and jelly sandwiches every day, complete with handwritten notes on paper napkins—"Have a good day! Mommy loves you!" This is not the time to be shy or self-deprecating or scared. Although, God knows it can be scary: Everyone is watching you, an opposing attorney is questioning you, and the man who once pledged to have and to hold till death do you part, who is most certainly alive and kicking, is now vowing to tell the truth, the whole truth, and nothing but the truth.

No matter how many hours of *Law & Order* you've consumed over the years, now is not the time to flex your legal muscles. Don't try to outsmart your ex's attorney with clever answers—you're paying your attorney for that. Your job is to show the judge what a loving, thoughtful, caring wife and mother, and all-around model citizen, you are. And as long as the judge has no knowledge of that one night in college you got stoned with those guys, and the only thing you remember is a shower curtain, baby oil, and two frat boys named Fred and Barney, then you should be able to pull it off, no problem. So, concentrate on coming off as your best, because that's what matters when the judge is making decisions that will affect your life from here forward.

Thoughts Going Through Your Head

When you enter the courtroom your head will be flooded with random thoughts. You're taking in everything, and everyone, with heightened sensitivity. Sure, you want to appear calm and collected, but the words inside your head make it feel like a three-ring circus has pulled into your frontal lobe and the show is about to begin.

Some things you may be thinking (and they're perfectly normal!):

- Does my ass look fat?
- He's definitely thinning on top, and I think I even see some gray.
- My attorney is better looking than yours.
- Was he just checking me out?
- Yes, this is a new suit, and yes, I paid for it with our joint checking account.
- Your attorney is wearing some really bad shoes.
- Just give me one look, one look that says you still feel something!
- The judge definitely likes me better.
- I recognize that suit . . . and it didn't used to be so tight on him.
- Am I allowed to say, "Objection, Your Honor"?
- Did my attorney just wheel in—on a handcart—four boxes of documents for our trial?
- How much is all of this costing me?

Yes, It's Really Real

This is an emotional day, as if that needed to be said. There's the whole, "I'm in court for my divorce" feeling.

This milestone makes the divorce real. Very real. For me, I don't think I ever felt like the whole divorce thing was real until I walked into that courtroom.

It's easy to get emotional on a day like today, because it's now officially before a judge. When another party is involved in deciding your fate, it can take on a certain gravity that you may not have felt before. Know that if you and your soon-to-be-ex can't work out the details, and you end up going to trial, you are going to get a big fat bill for it. Trials tack on serious hours for your attorney, and you pay dearly for that privilege. I hope that you won't need a trial, and that everything can be worked out between the two of you. If you do go to trial, listen to your attorney, dress appropriately, try to remember the long-term goal here, and if all else fails, call an SDS for moral support.

The Divorced Girls' Society
TOOLKIT

What to Wear for Milestone No. 3

My attorney recommended I look professional, "Like you're going to work," she told me. But in my office, jeans with holes patched over by bandannas counted as professional, so that wasn't much help. The morning of my first court appearance I selected what I thought was the perfect outfit: a slim black skirt, a crisp white shirt, and a pink blazer—slightly boxy, all business—that buttoned all of the way to the top. My daughter, the resident fashion consultant, gave me the double-thumbs down. She stepped into my closet and went to work, finally selecting a pale yellow cardigan with small pearl buttons. She let me keep the black skirt. By contrast, my daughter's selection made me look small, demure, almost fragile.

The pink jacket said, "Back off, I'm a career woman who chooses bright-colored clothes that are a size too large for me," while the pale yellow cardigan wondered innocently, "Why am I here in the courtroom? All I ever wanted was to be a good wife and mother." On second thought, my daughter did have a future in this fashion stuff. Her selection was perfect. And it took a five-year-old to see that.

What you wear is all about the message you want to send. Considering wearing the red silk shirt and short black skirt with your thigh-high stockings, the ones with the seam up the back of the leg, in hopes one look will send your ex running to you with open arms? Maybe not the best idea. That Laura Ashley dress that you think will tell the judge you're an old-fashioned woman who believes in family values and home-cooked pies? Think again. First and foremost, be yourself, be comfortable, and be confident. How you're feeling will speak volumes—although maybe not as loudly as the thigh-high stockings.

Milestone No. 4: You and/or Your Ex Have Significant Others

Yeah, you're going to have to face this eventually.

Depending on where this falls in the timeline of the milestones, it can either be a shrug-inducing nonincident, or it can set you back about six months in terms of emotional progression. If your ex's significant other is the reason you are now Sally Single Gal, then that would suggest that her existence may have been known for a while, in which case you may have folded this event into your other grieving moments. You may have also burned her likeness in effigy, thought about your ex and "her" when you were at your darkest points, wishing secretly that they would be swallowed whole by some Godzilla-like beast and chewed into bite-sized pieces. Let's hope you've gotten that out of your system, and that no small animals were harmed in the process.

Tips for Your SPEED-DIAL SISTERS

Don't instigate. When your friend begins dating, don't Google the guy to find out if there are outstanding warrants in six states. If her ex begins dating, don't Google the girl and then forward your friend a link to her *Girls Gone Wild* video premiere. While it's easy to believe that this is helpful to your friend—you are, after all, providing information that she should have—the fact is, it isn't helpful. It's stirring the pot, and there's enough in her life being stirred up right now without you adding to the brew.

Don't Ask, Don't Tell

Most likely, you and your ex will both be enjoying the dating life shortly (okay, *enjoying* may be overdoing it). As difficult as it may be to comprehend this concept, neither one of you owes the other an explanation (since, after all, you are now divorcing). In fact, once you're living separately, you may not have immediate knowledge of his personal life. Which is actually a good thing. I mean, his personal life has no bearing on you whatsoever, except as it relates to your children, and of course, they are to be protected and shielded from any and all adult nonsense (which includes dating and personal lives). His personal life has as much relevance to your life as the waitress serving you chicken wings at Fridays. Sure, you may know his address and that he picks your kids up every Wednesday at 6:00 P.M., but what he's doing on a daily basis and who he's doing it with? Really, none of your business. So don't ask. None of this, "Where were you last night at 3:00 A.M. when I called to see where you were taking the kids for dinner?" And the same goes for your social life. It's not necessary to explain that on your date last Saturday night you ordered the salmon and it was really too dry, but the dill sauce was great.

Because the two of you are now somewhat disconnected from one another, you may get knowledge of his new significant other quite by accident. Maybe you run into the two of them at a store in the mall (remember that scene in *When Harry Met Sally* when Harry is singing on the karaoke machine and his ex walks in?). It could be that awkward and even embarrassing (even if you're not singing "Surrey with the Fringe on Top"). Or it could make you feel relieved. Maybe you called the marriage quits and still feel guilty. The guilt monster is rearing its ugly head and, because you feel responsible, you're worried about his happiness, whether or not he'll pull through this okay. Seeing your ex with another woman might actually let you breathe that sigh of relief and give you permission to let the guilt monster return to the depths it came from.

However it happens, know that you should look at this event as a big step toward emotionally removing yourself from his life, and recognizing that his—and more importantly, your—life goes on after divorce. To be more specific, life goes on, love goes on, and we all continue to press on.

The Divorced Girls' Society
GOLDEN RULES

- Do acknowledge that this milestone is part of your recovery (no, not from that Oreo addiction, but from your relationship).
- Do focus on your dating life, not his. Pay no attention to his social life. Instead, pay attention to the guy in the transitional colonial living up the street who always stops and talks to you when you're out walking. The only social life that should matter is your own.
- Do keep your dating commentary to yourself—your children should not know that you are even the mildest bit perturbed at the thought of your ex getting jiggy with it with a new woman. Don't rub it in your ex's face if you start dating first—even if your date is the hottest thing since Tabasco.
- Don't spend your time imagining what your ex and his new gal pal are doing together.
- Don't probe for details. It's none of your business what your ex is now doing in his spare time. Even if it is with the aerobics instructor from your step and burn class on Friday mornings.

Milestone No. 5: The Final Document Is Sent, Stamped, Notarized, and Wax-Sealed by the County—It's Official

The duality of this monumental milestone is almost ironic. It's over. And yet the conflicting emotions continue to come.

One part of you wants to break out the champagne and make a toast—to you, your future, and the resilience you demonstrated throughout the entire ordeal. This is the official beginning of your new life. You've probably already made great strides toward becoming a single gal, but this seals the deal. It signifies the closing of the first book of your life (aptly named "Once Upon a Time I Was Married"); and this moment also shelves it, nicely and carefully, on the bookshelf in the section marked "History." It also heralds the beginning of the second book—totally different from the first—which you can now open and begin enjoying.

On the other hand, this is the ending of your old life. It's sad. Really, really sad. Whereas before you had a process to work through, milestones to pass, and a goal in mind, now you just have every day as an unmarried woman. And real life is never as exciting, or motivating, as an ordeal. So in addition to feeling sad, you may also be feeling a little deflated, the same way you feel when the fabulous week on the beach is over and it's time to head home and face the daily grind (not that divorce is a day, no less a week, at the beach).

Will it be bittersweet? Of course. You wouldn't be that modern, smart, capable-yet-sensitive gal if you didn't acknowledge it for the mixed bag of emotions that it is. What you should focus on, though, is accepting it as the start of something totally new. And don't you love the idea of new? Like writing in a journal whose spine hasn't been cracked? Or driving a car off of the lot and inhaling that brand new car smell? Your life is about to start anew. That's a gift for many. And you've just had it handed to you in a nice neat package by the county clerk.

DIVORCED GIRLS' SOCIETY TENETS

✓ These five divorce milestones are all a giant step toward your future and your new life.

✓ Keeping the house means keeping it nice—don't neglect your home-maintenance responsibilities, even if your ex assumed most of them previously.

✓ Your lawyer plays a big part in these steps—make sure she knows what's important to you, and make sure you're letting her do the heavy lifting.

✓ Significant others should only matter if they're in your life—anyone else is meaningless to you.

One Step Forward, Two Steps Back . . .

Forward progress gets everything closer to its finish, but the road to the end is sometimes filled with potholes, exits that you erroneously take when you should keep on going, rest stops, and detours. As with any trip, a good map, a reliable engine to keep you moving, and a level head can help propel you on that right path to the end. But sometimes, things just don't go that way. Because this is life, and it wasn't written by Rand McNally.

Those navigational annoyances are the divorce equivalent of setbacks. Like potholes, they can leave you shaken (the unexpected setback); like a wrong turn off an exit, they can irritate you and delay your arrival (the setbacks that pile up); and like a detour, they can bring about an element of the unknown that causes unexpected stress (hitting the wall). But knowledge is power here, and this is also one area where your team of experts, especially your attorney, should be playing a major role. The more you know about what to expect with setbacks, the faster, smoother approach you will make to the finish line.

The Unexpected Setback

It's the pothole you weren't expecting, because you're already way ahead of schedule; you're doing eighty, and you haven't seen a state trooper for the last 140 miles. You will be especially vulnerable at times like this, when you may not even be feeling vulnerable. "Huh?" you ask. Picture this: Things are chugging along just fine and dandy; the whole divorce process seems to be moving along quite seamlessly now. You've had numerous meetings with your attorney, and the parties seem to be agreeing more than not. You interact with your ex, and you actually find yourself saying hello without gritting your teeth. You've taken a few turns on the depression-go-round, but you are not grabbing the brass ring for an extra ride. And then all of a sudden, wham! Setback city.

Maybe it's something like your ex calls and asks if you wouldn't mind if he switched next month's visitation with the kids. "I'm taking Candy to Cabo San Lucas for a week of sun and relaxation," he explains, and she has seven thong bikinis, so they'd like to stay for seven days to make sure they all get used.

Sun and relaxation? Who the hell has time for sun and relaxation when you're going through a divorce? How can he think of thongs and margaritas when he should be thinking about funding a college education? (Of course, now the only thing *you* can think of is Candy in her thong bikinis.) "Sure," you answer, because the change in visitation really doesn't affect your schedule, as you had nothing planned those days anyway. And so, what started out as a great day—that guy you had coffee with last Sunday just e-mailed you to see if you wanted to go to the sold-out Cirque du Soleil show—goes decidedly into the toilet. The only acrobatics you can envision are the upside-down moves that require the removal of Candy's thong. Things go downhill from there.

Woe is you, the woman at home in her cold house, snuggling under an afghan while other people sun their buns. How sad you are, with no plans to speak of except defrosting the freezer and those belly-dancing classes at the Y. That pit in your stomach is best relieved with a quart of Häagen Dazs and a bag of Doritos. Might as well pack on the pounds to keep you warm during the long winter, hunkered down under the afghan in your cold house.

Stop. Stop right there. Those belly-dancing classes— they were one of the activities you decided to pursue several chapters ago. You've always wanted to belly dance, ever since your childhood fascination with *I Dream of Jeanie*. And snuggling under an afghan? You're not just snuggling, you're reading all of those books you'd put aside for years and promised to get back to some day. Well, guess what? This is some day.

Still, all of this is cold comfort when faced with your husband's spectacular vacation plans. And that's why we call this a setback.

MANTRAS **to get you through the day**

When life gives you lemons . . .

Chutes and Ladders, Divorce Style

Remember playing Chutes and Ladders as a kid? You'd roll the dice, make your move, and end up several spaces ahead of where you started. Good for you, you were on your way to winning. But then there were times when you'd roll the dice, and, through no fault of your own, end up on the space with the chute. And the chute was bad news. A one-way ticket down. A slip backward. All of that progress you made, shot to hell.

Setbacks are a lot like that staple of childhood game playing. But back then you didn't give up. You didn't throw the dice at your brother, declare yourself a lifetime loser, and never venture into the land of board games again.

What's important to remember here is that in order to have a setback, you have to have made progress in the first place. And you were. Making progress, that is. So see how far you've come? If you're sliding down a chute, at least that means you're still in the game. And that's how you should look at your own divorce setbacks. Remember when you were just beginning this adventure we call divorce? Belly dancing was but a glimmer in your eye. Now you can shimmy and shake with the best of them.

So have that Häagen Dazs, and let yourself feel what it's like to be back where you were months ago. And

then remind yourself that months ago you didn't know
how far you could go. Now you do. And you can get
there again. Just keep rolling those dice.

The Setbacks That Pile Up

Setbacks can be one-offs, or a highway pile-up that makes
L.A. rush hour feel as uneventful as the cafeteria line for
tater-tot surprise. Imagine this: You're already in a slump,
you're not feeling good about a lot of things in your life,
and moving backwards actually feels consistent with
everything else you're going through. That's the defeat-
ist in you showing her sad, pathetic self, and it happens
when the setbacks get so numerous, so frequent, it's hard
to even know which direction is forward. It's like when
you're on a diet and you give in to your weakness and
break out the Cheetos. Shortly after, you've convinced
yourself that the giant Toblerone bar is also a good idea;
after all, you already downed the Cheetos and have the
orange fingers to prove it. So, while you're on a roll,
why not wash it all down with a 2003 Cabernet? And
nothing goes better with Cabernet than a bucket of Ken-
tucky Fried Chicken. Before long you're on a fast train
to Bloatsville, because each slip-up erodes your resolve
and enables the next. You've been steered off course, and
the default response is to remain off course, since you're
already there and the scenery isn't so bad.

Now replace Cheetos and Toblerone bars with a series
of divorce events that all go the opposite way you had
planned or hoped they would. You may have a bad
meeting with your attorney, maybe you've just realized
that Mr. I-Don't-Want-to-Be-Married-Anymore just used

your Visa for a $1,500 out-patient hair-plug treatment, and he's also decided that the family dog belongs with him. The bad news just keeps piling up, and you're having a tough time thinking positively. This is when you are quite vulnerable to taking a step back (or more). Signs of discouragement are everywhere.

You can't control other people's actions, and often you can't control circumstances that affect you, but you can control how you react to them. Call in your pep-squad friend; she is the best qualified to help pull you up by the straps of your strappy leather slingbacks and get you marching forward once again. Double up on the belly-dancing lessons and the determination that got you shaking your hips in the first place. Instead of reminding yourself what life was like before you separated, remind yourself how difficult those first weeks were—and how far you've come.

Understand that some setbacks are out of your control (the ex and the hair-plug fiasco? You didn't cause that). What you can control is your mental attitude about pushing forward (and you may want to also cancel the authorized-user feature of your once-shared Visa card). Piled-on setbacks can pack a punch to both your willingness to fight on and your emotional stamina. To help diffuse how strongly the disappointment-flame burns, take a big, deliberate step forward in a positive direction. Do it big, do it loud.

The following ideas for big steps in the right direction will remind you that you are on a forward-moving journey, with a finish line up ahead, and your focus is on getting there quickly, as painlessly and hassle free as possible (with little collateral damage).

The Divorced Girls' Society
TOOLKIT

Big Steps Forward

- Tell your ex in an e-mail that you would like every and all communication to go through your attorney.
- Do an internal assessment of your grief stages and identify what you've already gone through and what you should expect.
- Call your attorney several months into your divorce and remind her about your feelings on some of the big issues that you feel strongly about. When she hears your passionate plea, this will embolden her to be extra forceful and legally hawkish on the issues that you are most concerned about. Normally, I don't encourage proactive phone calls to your attorney, but in this case, it's money well spent. Remember, she's a busy attorney; she may not have your case at the top of her mind. So it's your job to get her as concerned about the big things as you are.
- Identify the things that are important to you about the outcome of your divorce. Maybe you want the flexibility of moving to another state? Maybe you want to make sure Junior has a full financial ride to his choice of colleges (and none of them have the word "junior" in them). Make the list, and keep it in full view (tape it to your bathroom mirror), and let those goals keep you motivated and charged up about getting to the end of this journey.

Tips for Your SPEED-DIAL SISTERS

You've been doing your job, offering positive reinforce-ment when needed and a swift kick in the ass when required, and always lending a willing ear. But just when you think she's stepped away from the ledge and things are moving forward, your divorcing girlfriend has a setback. And that means you have to listen, for the 234th time, to how her soon-to-be-ex insists that he gets the snow blower, even though the only thing he blew during the ten years of their marriage was his nose. Is it time to put your foot down and tell her to snap out of it and stop feeling sorry for herself?

No, it's not. There's no statute of limitations on being a friend, and you're in this for the long haul, even if that means letting her rehash the last month's conver-sations with her attorney so many times you're consid-ering charging your friend by the hour, too.

So how do you get her back on track? Remind her of the progress she's made. That night she went to the movies alone? Didn't she tell you how nice it was not to have to listen to her soon-to-be-ex chomping on Milk Duds for two hours? And those bikram yoga classes that have made her appreciate a good sweat even though her ex insisted no woman looked good with pit stains? She's really come so far, and it's your job to convincingly reinforce her progress.

Hitting the Wall (It's Mighty Big, and You Forgot Your Rappelling Equipment)

There is another particularly frustrating setback. It's called hitting a wall. There's no detour, seemingly no alternative path. Nothing but those orange blinking signs set smack-dab in the center of the road, a dead stop. This abrupt force stops your progress, leaving you frustrated, anxious, and with a bruised nose, depending on how hard and fast you plowed into the wall. The wall is a tough one, because it's not any one instance, any single circumstance, that sets you on your ass. It's the accumulation of everything going on in your life, and when it piles up it looks way too big to climb over, go around, or dig through. And unless you happen to have rappelling equipment with you (spiked shoes and some sturdy rope), there doesn't seem to be much hope. Don't do this one alone. Hopefully you have yourself a therapist by this point, and that therapist will come in handy right about now. She'll make that wall into a molehill, or at the very least play trail guide and set you on your path again.

Tracking Progress to Prevent Setbacks

When you want to make a large purchase, you start saving in advance. You track your growing bank account. If you want to squeeze into that bikini by summer, you set a goal and monitor your progress. The lesson here? If you know where you need to go, you need to know how you're doing before you can get there. And because life can be divided into twelve easy pieces—months—and each piece into four smaller pieces—weeks—using a calendar to chart your progress during divorce is a great idea.

So get yourself a plain household calendar—and make it something you'll enjoy looking at (those calendars with the cute, fuzzy kittens chasing balls of yarn are good—how can you be depressed watching Fluffy at play?).

Mark down the day you and your ex separated, and then mark one year after that; call that your end date, for now anyway. At the very least, one year after your separation a lot will have happened; hopefully, you'll be able to see the light at the end of the divorce tunnel.

Each month select one day out of that month (say, the second Monday) and write down what you've done to make forward progress. Also write down what you have identified as setbacks, no matter how small or inconsequential. The whole idea here is a lot like those chore charts designed to reward children for doing things like making their beds, picking up their toys, and walking the dog—all of the things we do without the star stickers and call-out boxes exclaiming "Great job!" Here's your chance to give yourself those stickers, and maybe reward your progress with more than a self-adhesive A+.

An example of your progress: You came across a box of old photos and flipped through them, smiling and laughing the whole time (except the pictures with that haircut you gave yourself with the Flowbee; okay to toss those).

An example of a setback: You're on a business trip in Chicago, and the restaurant in your hotel is the very same one you and your ex dined at many years ago. You wax nostalgic over the memories, break out your cell phone, and call your ex. When he answers, you say, "I double-dog dare you to recall the name of that restaurant on the corner of Delaware and Michigan Avenues." You are so caught up in the moment that you fail to realize that the long silence on the other end of the phone isn't due to bad cell reception. He replies with, "I don't recall. And this is a bad time." This would be a setback. Not a major one, no immediate bad consequences, but consider what you've just done: Not only have you revealed to him that you are living in the past, it sets you up to appear soft and sentimental. Not the kind of image you want to be projecting. This could put your ex on the offensive, and he could take advantage of you.

Beware, Trouble Ahead:
Sex with an Ex

The fact that two-thirds of the word "sex" is "ex," in and of itself should be enough warning to avoid this one. The letters are so intertwined, it's almost hard to discern where one ends and the other begins.

Besides setting you *on* your back, it just plain-old sets you back. Honestly, what are the benefits here? Sex diffuses stress, but so does a trip to the gym. It's a great distraction, but so is trying to run a six-minute mile. And you don't feel deserted when the guy on the treadmill next to you up and leaves without a kiss goodbye.

You're a big girl; you know that sex is a complicated thing. And complications should actually be on the short list of things you must avoid. I mean, isn't life complicated enough right now? What with learning how to juggle your job, single parenting, and trying your best to avoid that creepy dude in marketing who just discovered you're single, there's no room in your life for sex with an ex (or that creepy dude in marketing).

Rest assured, divorcing gal, these are short-term calamities. As with all setbacks, they are temporary, and fixable. By tracking the good and the bad, you have lessons to remember. Read your setbacks and progress meters regularly, to remind you of what you are working toward. And to ensure you don't make the same mistakes twice.

Some setbacks are unavoidable. Some can be avoided, or at least controlled, if you take proactive steps. Don't put yourself in complicated or vulnerable situations, and remember to work with your well-paid, and highly qualified team of experts—attorney, therapist, and friends—to mitigate (or altogether avoid) the risk of setbacks.

DIVORCED GIRLS' SOCIETY TENETS

✓ Don't cave in! This is still war, and you are still on the front lines. Enlist additional troops if you think your stamina is weakening or your strategy needs a reassessment.

✓ Remind yourself what you want out of this divorce, and keep that reminder front and center.

✓ Measure your progress, and reward your steady moves forward; don't harp on the moves backward, and keep planning ahead.

✓ You're not paying your team of experts to warm the bench—get them out there defending you and pushing for your best interests.

13

If the Berlin Wall Can Cease to Serve Its Purpose, so Can Your No-Fly Zone

At some point—after six months, after a year—
it's over. The divorce is finalized, and you're
no longer linked to the man you once believed
would be your happily ever after. And that's
when you'll realize that it's time to move on,
time to cease enforcing all of the rules that made
the grueling process of divorce bearable. Those
principles were put in place to protect you while
you were at your most vulnerable, developed
in recognition of the significant emotional stuff
you had to deal with. But you can't use them
forever.

This is the tough-love portion of the book, and
it needs to be said: The tools that allowed you
to get through your divorce in a focused and
undistracted way must be retired. They've out-
lasted their usefulness. You can't keep living like

you're still adjusting to your new state. Every divorcing woman deserves to be cut some slack, that's a fair argument. But there are time limits on the slack. And while I won't tell you that you need to start living your life within one year of the event, I will tell you that the longer you wait, the more you miss out on. And don't you want to move on? If you're reading this book, you've certainly decided that there's got to be more to life than a future thinking of yourself as the divorced woman. The only way to do this is to get back into the swing of things, back to the new normal that is your life. A world where you're single, and that's okay; where you have a new life filled with other—better—choices, partners, and viewpoints.

Lifting the No-Fly Zone

Believe it or not, there will come a time when you've had enough—enough of thinking about divorce, enough of feeling guilty, enough of the past. You'll realize that you have a new life to explore and live, and that your divorce-management strategies are no longer needed. You'll feel differently about subjects and situations that previously may have elicited strong, emotional reactions from your formerly frail and emotionally uncertain self. That ski trip that my ex had the nerve to invite my sister's husband on four months after he announced he was done with our marriage? Sure, that was totally insensitive, even unacceptable behavior on his part. My brother-in-law was told, in no uncertain terms, that he was not allowed to go skiing with the enemy. But two years later the invite was extended again, and I gave it the green light. It no longer seemed like such a big deal.

You may want to rekindle old friendships, pick up the phone and start up a dialogue with people who had been blacklisted while the divorce was taking place. Ex-mothers-in-law are good places to start. After all, your children still need their Grammy, and would it hurt to give her a quick check-in? She'll probably love hearing your voice, and be relieved (and impressed) that you have such a positive mental outlook on life after such a big blow. Think of it as your coming-out party of sorts. You've been avoiding some people for a while, putting them into the enemy's camp. Now that you're well on your way, and living this fabulous new single life, it might be a nice opportunity to share your good fortune with those who have known you, and those with whom you may have fallen out of touch.

The realization that I no longer needed to be protected from those not in my inner circle happened sort of by accident. My daughter was in New Jersey with her grandparents and a phone call to their house was answered—not by my daughter as usual (they had caller ID, so they knew that it was me)—by my ex-mother-in-law. She started off cautiously, "Vicki? Hi!" At first I cowered at the thought of talking with her again. After all, we hadn't spoken in nearly a year, and who knew what she had heard about the divorce? I didn't know if I should assume the worst—that my husband had shared all of my nasty habits and the deep dark secrets of our twelve-year marriage. Had my ex convinced her that I was an utterly unlikable woman with ice-water running through my veins? Or did he play the poker face for the past year and not disclose any details about the unraveling of our marriage?

There was no way to know. So I did something quite simple, something I couldn't have imagined doing twelve months before. I took a deep breath and picked up where we had left off. I actually smiled as we spoke, because honestly, it was nice to hear her voice again. Sure, she may have heard some horror stories about me, she may even have changed her feelings for a daughter-in-law she once doted on, but it didn't matter. I knew how I felt about her, knew I had missed her in my life, and was grateful to have a chance to speak with her on the phone, even if by accident.

When it's time to lift the No-Fly Zone, you'll know. You won't fear running into your ex's colleague, the one you used to go out to dinner with at least once a month. Seeing his sister in the line at the grocery store won't send you running toward the dairy aisle muttering something about lactose intolerance. Instead, a person whom you used to view as a defector will simply become a familiar face, a familiar face who, more than likely, will smile at you and await your response. And you know what? Chances are, if you've made it this far, you'll smile back.

Retiring the Get-Out-of-Jail-Free Cards

Remember when it was okay to walk out on a movie just because the sight of Austin Powers in his glasses made you remember the day you spent three hours at LensCrafters helping your ex pick out the perfect pair of wire rims? Well, that's not okay anymore. Everyone has cut you the slack you needed to make it another day, but those days are over. Time to enter the world of the living, and in that world you don't get out of jail free. You sit in a cement cell on a mildewed cot and wonder when you're going to get your one phone call, while your cell-mate stares at you with hungry eyes, licks her lips, and growls something that sounds like "filet mignon."

The Divorced Girls' Society
GOLDEN RULES

- Do help other DGS members in their time of need—remember, you've been there, so you know what she's going through. Give back—keep the DGS circle strong.
- Do reconnect with those who you may have relegated to the No-Fly Zone over the past year.
- Don't concern yourself with people from the past whom you won't be back in touch with now that the divorce is final. Life moves on for all of us—suffice it to say that they've probably moved on too.
- Don't be surprised if, at some point, your relationship with your ex transcends the BS that's taken place over the past year (or more). You may actually start thinking about him as a good guy, even though things didn't work out.

I haven't wanted to put a timeline on anything because we're all different, we all have our own timeline. This is the one area where I'll come out and say it: The Get-Out-of-Jail-Free Cards have a one-year expiration date. Your divorce may still be ongoing, but you shouldn't have to invoke any special treatment in order to get through the day anymore. Like at the family gathering a year and a half after the divorce, when a cousin you don't much care for starts talking about her own divorce, thinking you are the ideal confidante, now that you've both shared in the gloom and doom. Know what? As much as you may want her to talk to the hand—because you can't stomach the thought of sharing divorce war stories with this person—remember that maybe it's time you think about others, especially others who are going through what you just endured. Pour her a glass of wine and lend her a much-needed ear. You may want to tell her about that helpful little card that you were thinking about pulling out. There is a statute of limitations on being an unpleasant divorcing woman, and eventually manners and being nice start to count again, so make Emily Post proud.

It's Reassuring to Know That London Fog Makes a Nice Burberry Knockoff

That khaki overcoat you look so good in? You can don it now, because if you're going to go through the pain and hassle of divorce, you may as well get something out of it. And in this case, what you can get out of it is a little good introspection and a lot of good lessons. It's time for the postmarital postmortem.

You've endured a lot of heavy-hitting experiences over the last year, so take advantage of them. Get out that magnifying glass and stare closely, because once you put yourself and your relationship under the glass, you should be able to see the whats, whys, whens, and hows of how it came to this a lot more clearly. What you find might not be pretty, it may even make you shake your head and wonder, *What the hell was I thinking*? Of course, this will only work if you can take an objective detective-like approach to examining your relationship and, more importantly (gulp), yourself.

For those of us with need-to-know personalities, doing a marital postmortem is a necessary exercise. And you'll know you're ready when you begin to admit and recognize some of your own shortcomings. It doesn't hurt if you can also consider your ex's personality in a way that doesn't send you into a fit of rage. The postmortem is all about being honest—brutally honest—with yourself.

MANTRAS to get you through the day

There's always room for improvement.

For me, when I thought about what I could have done differently, a few things entered my mind. For one, I probably could have used an extra helping of sensitivity the day my ex got into that car accident and my first question wasn't "Are you hurt?" but "You were supposed to meet me at the train at 6:30. How the hell am I supposed to get home now?" And for him, he probably could have been more accepting and less brooding when we ate in restaurants that I preferred, but where he tsked and sighed as he pushed the chicken tiki masala around his plate. It's not one or two events that go wrong that lead to the end of your marriage; it's probably a culmination of them. But you can identify patterns of behavior that manifest themselves in situations, which collectively add up to the big reason why you two are not married anymore.

The point of this exercise is to take stock of who you are. What is it about you—your relationship skills, your emotional quotient—that you might want to improve? If you were a sports team, this would be where you sit in the locker room at halftime while the coach points out the missed opportunities to leverage your strengths, the plays that weren't executed as well as they could have been. But in this case, you're the coach and the player, so you have the benefit of not only taking the time to identify where things should be done differently in the future, but of being the one who can actually change the way the game is played. You have the ability to assess where you are as a person and a romantic partner and determine how you'll make improvements moving forward. And all this without the musty locker-room smell and athlete's foot.

Need some questions to help you get to the answers? Try these:

- What did I learn about myself throughout this process? Has it changed how I deal with conflict, react to criticism, communicate my emotions, etc.?
- Knowing myself as I do now, what relationship advice would I give myself moving forward?
- How would I describe who I am today, versus who I thought I was one year ago?
- How can I continue to leverage this experience in the future?

Sometimes, the only way to see things clearly is to step back for a new perspective. But when you're objective enough to begin the postmortem process, please keep in mind that it's not about identifying your ex's each and every fault. Sure, compare your traits with his and evaluate what it was about him that was incompatible

with you. This is constructive, not because you can alpha-
betize all of the ways he ever annoyed you, but because
the next time around you'll have a better idea of what
you can live with, and what you want to live without.
Maybe his idea of rejecting gender stereotypes meant
you were the one cleaning out the gutters; or that to him
being generous during sex was when he tossed you his
used towel to clean up after. If you're in the right frame
of mind, you can look back at that and have a good
laugh. You can also use this information to help assess
what personality traits complement yours best.

What Your GIRLFRIEND *Is Thinking*

Okay, I'll admit it (and don't think I'm a bitch): This Is
Great! She Should Have Gotten Divorced Ages Ago!

Yes, it's nice to have her back. I like the fact that
we're talking on the phone more, that our conversations have a greater level of honesty and sensitivity,
that we're planning vacations together again. In some
perverse way, our friendship was the beneficiary of her
misfortune. I got to play the role of caretaker, sensitive
best friend, provider of sage wisdom, and purveyor of
one-liners that made her smile. Sure, it made me feel
good to make her feel good, but it's time our friendship moved on as she moves on. While it was nice to
be there when she needed me, it's also nice to have her
back on her feet. And that's how I prefer her. Because
now that she's dating, she's invested in several slinky
pairs of high-end footwear, and we just happen to
share the same shoe size.

You Didn't Think I'd Leave out the Subject of Men, Did You?

Of course I think about men. In a way, I feel like I'm twelve again, discovering the opposite sex for the first time. Though when I was twelve, if a guy was good at Atari, that counted for a lot. But I do have some clear ideas in my head of the kind of qualities I am now seeking. Qualities that have become more important to me now that I've gone through my divorce.

Whereas before I wanted ambition, now I wanted someone with lots of interests. I was also looking for someone who was comfortable talking about sensitive subjects. Think of it like a Chinese menu: Once you've spent the time to decipher what was once undecipherable, the more you know about your choices, the more educated your choices, and the more enjoyable the meal. If you've never tried the poo poo platter because, in translation, it was something of a turnoff, you won't know that it's better than the lo mein. But the more you've experienced, the better choices you'll make the next time around. I'm not saying that guys are like Chinese food (although I have met Peking ducks with more personality than some guys I've met online), but leveraging your divorce experiences, as well as all of your past relationships, can go a long way toward helping you make better choices with the men in your life.

So, while the only six packs I've seen around thirty-eight-year-old men are the ones with Budweiser on the label, I do look for characteristics in men that I never would have even been aware of before. I have a different set of standards, all thanks to my experience as a divorced woman. Am I more discerning? Possibly. Am I wiser? Definitely.

What Your GIRLFRIEND *Is Thinking*

It wasn't until I hung up the phone one afternoon after talking with Vicki that I realized that we didn't mention the D-word during our entire call. Sure, I knew she was probably meeting with her lawyer to go over the final settlement agreement, and I was positive that there'd no doubt been moments of frustration with her soon-to-be-ex, but the topic of her divorce no longer dominated the conversation. And that's when I knew that life would go on. It might not be exactly like it was before her husband made his announcement, but it wouldn't be so different either. Our friendship was intact, we were making plans for the future—*she* was making plans for the future—and it was exciting.

Now I look forward to hearing about all of the new things she's doing, the possibilities that lay ahead of her. I know that no matter where she ends up, or even if she just stays put in Richmond, there will be all sorts of new things we'll go through together. Like her first serious relationship. (I can't even begin to imagine what that conversation will entail, although I'm sure there's all sorts of etiquette I'll have to follow . . . can I ask about her new sex life?) But one thing will stay the same, and that's the fact that we're still best friends.

Your Life No Longer Resembles a Lifetime Movie (and You're Way More Put Together Than Meredith Baxter Birney Ever Was)

Oh, the drama. There was lots of it while you went through your divorce. Hopefully that's all over. In fact, if you're dating, you might have left drama behind and entered new territory: romantic comedy. Even if you started out a tad leery of the opposite sex, by now you should have replaced the old dreaded D-word (divorce) with a new D-word that actually has you feeling a little optimistic—dating. Dating is now a regular part of your life, incorporated into the rest of your busy schedule, like soccer practice for your six-year-old and grocery shopping on Saturdays. Sure, you've probably spent time with your share of guys who fall well below the bar—but how great that you've set it so high!

Having a romantic interest is more than a pleasant distraction in your postdivorce life. It can help reaffirm some of those things you may have stopped believing in when your marriage ended. You may have given up on multiple orgasms, a hot cup of coffee handed to you in bed each morning, or someone to lend a hand at dinnertime. Men come in so many shapes and sizes, who's to say that the next significant other in your life might not have personality traits that you had long ago convinced yourself were just not part of the male DNA makeup. You may be pleasantly surprised.

I know I certainly was. A few short months after my divorce was final, I met a guy who, on paper and in person, appeared to be my exact opposite. He loved dogs, rode motorcycles, preferred spending the day outdoors identifying animal tracks on his three-acre wooded lot in rural Virginia, and sported some serious body art. Were these turnoffs? Not at all. Just interests I never thought about, which would suggest to me that I'd not be a suitable companion to this outdoorsy fella whose nightstand reading material included *Rifleman* magazine stacked up next to calculus textbooks. Yet, I was intrigued by this rugged, independent thinker with a penchant for tractors and stray animals. I wanted to give it a chance, because while he didn't fit into any category stereotypes I typically assigned people, there was something about him that I wanted to get to know better.

What I wondered as I got to know him was: Why was he so completely contrary to the conservative, image-conscious materialist who I, for so long, was convinced was my match? And it dawned on me: That was the criteria set by the predivorce me, and I had already spent fifteen years with one of those. I now cared more about getting to know people who challenged me, who encouraged me to explore new things about myself, who were an unexpected and positive change from my normal life. Now, pulling dog hair off my cashmere sweaters and spending afternoons hiking the Blue Ridge Mountains is routine. And getting my hot coffee in bed each morning (among other things) gives me renewed faith in men and their DNA makeup.

I attribute my ability to be more enlightened about my choice of partners to having gone through my divorce, and having done a lot of soul searching when I realized I wasn't going to be partners with my ex, the person I thought I'd be partners with forever. I realized, after all of that, that certain things were not important to me anymore. Moreover, I now expected certain things from any future partners. Which is what happens when you evaluate things at age twenty-two versus at age thirty-eight. No, age doesn't presume intelligence, but your experiences can help shape what your preferences are, and things gain or lose importance as you grow and become more experienced.

Just because you've called off the military police, doesn't mean you should completely forget what happened to you these past few months. No, you need to remember all of the things you've learned about yourself, your life, and your new choices as you move ahead. But you can't do that unless you step out from behind the protective walls and guarded environment you've been ensconced in during your divorce. Like the groundhog on February second, the world is waiting for your emergence, to see what you will do, as the new and improved single gal. Take off the pith helmet and bulletproof vest, fluff your hair, pop a breath mint, and get back into that thing you used to refer to as your life.

DIVORCED GIRLS' SOCIETY TENETS

✓ When the war is over—and it will be—make sure all parties know they can go back to their normal life. That includes you.

✓ You can't use "I'm going through a divorce" as an excuse forever.

✓ A little introspective examination can be revealing: It's okay to want to know why your marriage ended, and examine both your, and his, psyche for clues and answers.

✓ Remember, you're an evolved woman. Don't be surprised if you start making choices that will surprise even you.

There's a Light at the End of the Tunnel, and for Once It's Not a Two-Ton Locomotive Gunning Straight for You

I knew I'd made it when I lay in my bed awake at night and I wasn't crying about the past, but planning for the future. A future which seemed totally open and without any limitations. And it was all mine; it was all about me, me, me. My sleepless nights were now about what to do next, where to go, who to do it with. They were also, occasionally, about the unidentified noise in the kitchen, and wondering if the car door I just heard slam outside was a predator on his way inside my home. But an alarm system was $1000 well spent, and it didn't require feeding, laundry, and emotional maintenance like my former security system.

Who Knew That Your New Life Was So Good?

Sure, I was excited about what lay ahead. But it took my friends to see that this was actually a much bigger deal than I had realized. When you're living your life, you don't have the perspective that an outsider might. The perspective about what a new life actually means. The improvement in my everyday existence became evident to me when a friend suggested we take a week and attend an all-women's sailing school. All my married friends had to negotiate the time, the money, and in some cases, the approval from their husbands. One friend also complained about an envious husband who also wanted to learn to sail—couldn't we do a coed school instead (that would be a big No)?

Me? In five short minutes I sent an e-mail to my ex explaining that I needed him to take our daughter those days, and that I was happy to trade off a similar number of days for him when he wanted to get away. Trip planned. I did my own budgeting over the next six months—no dinners out, and I temporarily suspended my cleaning service—to save the money. I could never have done that while married, knowing my ex's propensity for dining out and his Pigpen-like habits. Things were done on my terms, and the only one approving my decisions was me. Now the only thing I had to worry about was where to buy a skipper's hat and how to hoist a jib and a vodka tonic at the same time.

MANTRAS to get you through the day

Whew.

How to Tell That You've Crossed Over to the Other Side

It's happened. You've done it, and, damn it feels so good. What a long, strange trip it's been, but you've crossed over to the other side.

- You find a box of your ex's ski accessories: goggles, gloves, sport sunglasses, neck warmer. You clean the goggles, wash the fuzzy turtle and ski mask, fold them and stack the items in a nice pile—all that's missing is a big red bow—and give it back to your ex.

- You decide to not turn your engagement ring into a skull-shaped pendant—instead you keep it as-is and store it in a safe-deposit box for when your daughter's boyfriend is ready to pop the question.

- You're at a lunch with your coworkers and a smart-ass makes a disparaging remark about how a divorced woman he's dating should feel lucky to date him—considering she's already a one-time loser. You toss your great hair over your shoulder, give him your best killer smile, and ask innocently, "How are those herpes treatments going, Stanley?"

- You go to the company holiday party alone . . . but you don't leave that way.

Enjoying That New-Life Smell (and It Doesn't Require Monthly Payments or Proof of Insurance)

So many of us don't get the opportunity to start our lives anew. I knew this was big, I knew this was something that doesn't come along very often. And I was both scared and excited. When I talked with my friends about my anticipation and hesitation, so many of them expressed envy at my clean slate—all of that hope and promise of great things to come was making them green. And it helped me realize that I had to grab this opportunity and make the most of it, because it might not happen to me again (God willing).

Sure, there are times when the future seems overwhelming (something as harmless as thinking about my daughter starting kindergarten snowballed into middle school, high school, and of course the day she waves goodbye to me from her college dorm), but I try not to let the snowballs get too big, or else they'll run me over.

You've Come a Long Way, Baby!

Take stock of what's transpired; it's been a whirlwind, no doubt. Your roller-coaster ride is finally pulling into the end gate, so you can release the harness and breathe a sigh of relief.

The first time I dropped my child off at my ex's apartment, after secretly reveling in the fact that he was living in 1600 square feet of rental space, complete with particle-board kitchen countertops and wall-to-wall carpeting, I was actually happy that my daughter and her dad were planning a great day together, and I in turn was able to plan my own day—guilt free. How liberating to go off and do something on my own without the constant fear or worry about a babysitter, impatient neighbor, or any other caregiver who was waiting for my return. My daughter was with her dad, and I had the day to myself. This was the beginning of my realization that my life had this new aspect of freedom that I never considered before.

The Divorced Girls' Society
TOOLKIT

My, How Far You've Come!

Here's a fun exercise that will demonstrate the progress you've made.

List four or five big slices that make up the pie of your life: for example, work, family, friends, spirituality, and hobbies. In the left column, write down a few adjectives that describe what those things meant to you a year ago. In the right column, write down what they mean to you now. The meaning may have changed, but the fact that you have important components of your life hasn't.

Here's one of mine:

Family before My Divorce	Family after My Divorce
Loving	Loving
Happy	My Responsibility
Took for granted	Strong
	Closer
	Funny

You Know How to Bring Home the Bacon and Fry It Up in a Pan . . . But Wouldn't It Be Nice to Bring Home a Filet Mignon?

Now that I am the most important adult in my life, I can make serious commitments to my job. My career had always played second fiddle to my ex's startup business. So I never cared about the professional accolades, or the progress I was making. I was all about a moderate challenge, working nine to five, and getting a healthy paycheck without having to break a sweat. In hindsight, that seems so limiting. My ex's priorities were dictating my professional goals. Now, however, I can dive head-first into what my career passions are. I can work toward bigger goals and dedicate my brainpower, experience, and time to climbing that ladder.

Before my divorce, I worked as a consultant for a *Fortune* 200 financial-services organization. My hours were predictable, paycheck solid but without promise of growing, and the only positive reinforcement of my good work was that my contract was extended. I wasn't getting feedback that could help me long term, and I wasn't feeling like my career was moving forward. After my separation, I realized that my career mattered more than ever now—after all, my daughter was now primarily under my care. I didn't have a husband anymore, and although there were legal stipulations that required my ex to contribute, who was to say that would always be there? I now had to pay attention to my professional success, since there was more riding on it.

With that knowledge, I applied for an associate job at the company I was consulting at. After a math test that left me with crossed eyes for a week, and a psychological exam that left me feeling like a lonely introvert with sociopathic tendencies, I was offered a job. I took it, knowing it was the right next step for what was happening in my life, and would help both me and my daughter in the long term (and the stock purchase plan isn't too bad, either).

Tips for Your SPEED-DIAL SISTERS

Don't assume that when this is all over, your friend will want to celebrate with a big old cake and a bevy of Chippendale dancers. While divorce is a monumental event, the end of the process is more like a sputter than a bang. There are no blaring trumpets, just some paperwork that arrives in the mail. In fact, you might not even know when it's "officially" over. In Vicki's mind, the arrival of the legal documents was simply a confirmation, not a culmination. Sure, there are women who will want the whole divorce party, the loud boisterous celebration. But maybe your friend would really like to go out for dinner and share a toast, or maybe she'd just like you to come over with a movie and some Jiffy Pop. She may even just want to spend the evening alone, letting it all settle in. Whatever her preference, take your cues from your friend, and you can't go wrong.

Back to the Future

It is tempting to try and map out my future with the accuracy of a GPS system, to mistake planning for control. But thinking too far ahead can be paralyzing. Will I still be alone when I'm forty? Fifty? Sixty? Will my daughter have to move in to take care of Mommy, who's now on a first-name basis with hosts of the Home Shopping Channel, and developed a close personal relationship with Madame Lazara and her magic ball? Mmm, let's hope not.

Don't think too far ahead. After all, years ago when you were waltzing down the aisle toward marriage, could you even begin to imagine everything you've been through the past year? Probably not. So take things a few days, a few weeks, a few months at a time. Like the giant chocolate flourless cake your friends got for you the day your divorce became official, don't try to eat it all at once. You'll only make yourself sick and you'll forget to savor every single bite.

The French Don't Call a Map "Le Plan" for Nothing

As you've read along the way, planning is good. Planning gives you a direction, a guide toward the end goal. Know that nothing is written in stone, and plans are works in progress, to be adjusted and tweaked as needed. Plans, like maps, can also provide many directions to one end goal. Don't feel restricted by a plan; let it help you get to where you want to go.

If thoughts of an uncertain future bring on the same mouth-sweating reaction as the snake-eating episode of *Fear Factor,* then do this simple exercise to help make the uncertainty of your future seem less daunting.

First, make a list of all of the things that you feel pretty confident you can manage in the near future (your children, your house, your job). Then write down the things you don't have any clue about—events you know will creep up years down the line, but that you can't imagine beginning to tackle (retirement, daughter's wedding, your *second* wedding).

Finally, compare the two lists. Which one has the greatest impact on your near-term happiness? Which list do you have the greatest control over? Which column do you feel good about? Probably the near future. See, things aren't so bad after all, so stop stressing and start enjoying. You're in the driver's seat.

Near Future   **Years Down the Line**

_____
_____
_____
_____
_____

The Divorced Girls' Society
GOLDEN RULES

- Do get a financial planner. Especially if your settlement included a large asset or sum of money. While it may be tempting to charter that Lear jet to Vegas and give everyone in your party a botox treatment and some gambling loot, lay low on what to do with your new earnings until you've consulted a professional.
- Do thank your SDSs, mom, friends, and anyone else who helped you get through this and held your hand as you crossed over to the other side. They deserve a shout out, or more. Your army helped you win this war; now it's time to give out medals, commendations, maybe even a few purple hearts. The critical battles have been fought, redeployment is now in progress. Take your "band of sisters" out for a night of fancy

food and drink. Or, better yet, prepare it yourself and have the gang over. You couldn't have done it without them. Now you need to tell them that.

- Don't try to tackle all of your big plans at once. Remember, you've got your whole exciting life ahead of you. You don't need to cram it all into one month—no one's taking it away.

- Don't stress about an unexplained emotional twinge. A song on the radio comes on five months after the divorce is final, and Van Morrison's "Have I Told You Lately" sends you over the edge. You frantically reach into your purse to see if you still have those cigarettes from last month's girls' weekend to calm yourself with a nicotine drag. You're a wreck, and the dial can't be turned to talk radio fast enough. It's okay. Humans are complex creatures—especially us gals. A song, a movie, even a flavor of ice cream might remind you of your ex. If it happens, it's totally normal. (One caveat: If it's happening every other day, you may want to increase your therapy visits to more than twice a month.)

A Conclusion and a Beginning

I am enlightened, educated, smarter, better. And I know what I want more than I ever have in my life. Divorce isn't only about endings, it's about new beginnings. I know that after everything I've endured, all of the tears and pain and personal analysis, it's finally paid off. Life is clearer. The image of myself is sharper, more defined. Divorce didn't end my dream, it just forced me to come up with a new one. And who doesn't want a new dream that's bigger and better?

You won't literally wake up one day and BAM, so begins your new life. All of the pieces and parts that make up your life will be moving along at different paces, but you should definitely take a moment to recognize, and even celebrate, the fact that you are in a new and better place than before. Your life is now whatever you want it to be—the constraints of marriage and another adult (and all of the emotional turmoil that accompanies that) have gone away. And now, there's nothing in the way of you doing what you want, how you want, all on your terms. And the experience you've gained along the way can help inform all of the things you want to plan in your future. You know better, you've struggled and fought through the tough times, the emotional tsunamis, and the stressful legal matters. All of those things have made an impression on your psyche, and will influence your future.

You've become an honored member of the Divorced Girls' Society. Welcome to the club. We're glad you've arrived.

DIVORCED GIRLS' SOCIETY TENETS

✓ At the risk of sounding like a 1970s cigarette ad: You've come a long way, baby!

✓ Your friends will be green with envy—recognize that this is a really big deal, and new beginnings don't come along often in life.

✓ Use your experience to help make the most of your future. Did the divorce trials and tribulations make you realize that you are an unusually flexible and calm person? Maybe you should look into getting certified at yoga.

✓ The war is over, but you will always need your wingman and foxhole buddies. Make sure you continue to include them in your life, and make sure you are always there for them.

✓ The Divorced Girls' Society exists for a reason: We all need to know we're not alone. From the Speed-Dial Sisters who might very well need you to lend an empathetic ear one day, to the women who discover, as you did, that they're not immune to statistics, the Divorced Girls' Society provides solace and humility and humor. Carry your membership card with pride in the knowledge that you're one of us . . . and we're pretty damn amazing.

Index

About the Authors

Vicki King, left, is a senior brand manager with a *Fortune* 200 financial-services company. She's worked in magazine publishing, holding editorial positions at *Harper's Bazaar,* managing promotions at *The New Yorker* and *Condé Nast Traveler* and writing regular features for *The Mountain Times* in Killington, Vermont. She lives in Richmond, Virginia, with her daughter and one-eyed cat named Wolfie.

Jennifer O'Connell is the author of several novels, including *Bachelorette #1, Dress Rehearsal, Off the Record,* and *Insider Dating.* She also edited the anthology *Everything I Needed to Know about Being a Girl I Learned from Judy Blume.* She attended the Radcliffe Publishing Program and received her M.B.A. from the University of Chicago. A market-strategy consultant, Jennifer lives outside of Boston with her husband, two children, and a mouse-catching machine named Midnight.

Best friends since they met their freshman year at Smith College, Vicki and Jennifer have endured the trials and tribulations of first loves, first jobs, first marriages, and, now, a first divorce. Join the society at *www.divorcedgirls society.com.*